CHRISTIANITY
MATTERS.

HOW OVER TWO MILLENNIA THE MEEK AND THE MERCIFUL REVOLUTIONIZED CIVILIZATION— AND WHY IT NEEDS TO HAPPEN AGAIN

—— By: ——

DAVID T. MALOOF

Printed in the United States of America.

CATALOG:
Maloof, David T.
    Christianity Matters : How Over Two Millennia The Meek and The
    Merciful Revolutionized Civilization—and Why it Needs to Happen Again /
    David T. Maloof
p. cm.
Index Included

LCCN: 2016919009
70x7 Publishing, Rye, New York

ISBN: 978-0692804551

First Edition

——— FOR: ———

My wife and life partner Jean.

I am the author of this book.

In so many ways, she is the co-author of my faith.

Nothing that is worth doing can be achieved in our lifetime; therefore we must be saved by hope. Nothing which is true or beautiful or good makes complete sense in any immediate context of history; therefore we must be saved by faith. Nothing we do, however virtuous, can be accomplished alone; therefore we must be saved by love.

- REINHOLD NIEBUHR

—— CONTENTS ——

———— INDEX TO PERSONS PROFILED ————

—————— PREFACE ——————

A BRAWL IN AN IVY LEAGUE PUB.

T though perhaps not the first time among men of partial Irish descent, I owe whatever eternal salvation I may earn to the outcome of a bar room brawl.

It goes back to my student days at Columbia University in the late 1970's. An offensive lineman on the football team took exception to my conversation with a certain blond lass. Before I had time to realize what he was doing, he had drenched me in beer – a favor that I quickly and thoughtlessly reciprocated, notwithstanding the fact that I spotted him 70 pounds. Just as the swinging was about to begin, the Columbia pub manager, a scrappy post-graduate former Golden Gloves boxer named Bob Muzikowski, leapt over the bar and grabbed the big fellow – whom he evidently knew well from prior altercations – and suddenly, it was no longer my fight.

Not taking kindly to his new escort, the football player thrust his clenched fist through a window on the way out of the bar - and it didn't end there. Hours later, around 4 am and still drunk, he reappeared at Bob's dorm room door, grabbed him in his underwear, and reignited the fight. Half-asleep, and caught in a desperate choke hold, while rolling down the dorm steps, Bob only survived by biting into one of his assailant's fingers, thereby freeing himself.

The University threatened to expel the fellow – after all, he had assaulted a University employee. But, oddly, Bob would have none of that. Rather, in a remarkable act of Christian forgiveness, he insisted that the punishment be that the player who had assaulted him be allowed to remain in school, and work for him in the Columbia Pub.

But this story is supposed to be about *my* salvation, not his.

Some thirty years later, as it turns out, I was living in Connecticut, practicing international law and raising a family, when a friend invited me to attend a Christian men's spiritual breakfast group called The New Canaan Society.

It was not my cup of tea – a hundred men singing loud praise music at 7 am, waving their hands in the air like they were calling for a fair catch, testimonials of lives wasted and saved – way too much drama for me, a simple Catholic, on a Friday morning. As I exited the prayer service, intending never to return, I spotted a flyer. In a few weeks, the motivational speaker would be none other than the former Columbia pub manager, one Bob Muzikowski.

I was surprised to learn that Bob had become born again, overcome addiction, made a ton of money selling Northwestern Mutual Insurance policies, and along the way had started America's largest inner-city little league on Chicago's deadly South Side. Hollywood had even made a movie about him, called 'Hardball,' where he was played by Keanu Reeves.

And so I had to attend one more time.

After Bob's speech, I waited in line to say hello. It turned out that he had also bought a closed Catholic school building, and was now running a Christian high school for inner-city youth, called Chicago Hope Academy. He had also written a book called Safe at Home (2001), about the youth baseball league, and was signing them at the event.

Even before I reached the front of the line he gave a shout out to me – "Don't we know each other?" "Sure," came my reply, "You leapt over a bar at Columbia University and saved my life." "Of course, I did," he retorted, "It's all in the book." And so it was, *sans* my name.

Pope John Paul II said: "There are no coincidences." Rather, what passes as 'coincidence' is merely God whispering to us. And so I said to myself, if, 30 years after the fact, God was going to bring this now evangelical back into my life – even have me mentioned in his book, then maybe I should try to renew my own religious life.

So that was the new beginning.

I was married to a woman whom I still adored, my law firm was chugging along well, my children were growing beautifully, my second career coaching my daughter and son to slightly above average outcomes in youth sports was winding down, and I wanted more out of life.

Always a believer, it made sense to me at this point in time to start living out the dedication in Muzikowski's book:

Preach the Gospel at all times.
If necessary, use words.

Right at that moment in time, as fate would have it, my own Catholic Church in Connecticut was making headlines - of the wrong kind. The pastor had been bilking the well-to-do congregation of large sums of money for his personal use, to the level that he was soon under arrest, and later died in jail. The Diocese responded by sending us one of their best – a truly faith-filled new pastor – but he really needed help in this crisis.

So several of us went to the new pastor and asked him if we could revitalize the parish men's group. For over a decade after that, I ran that group, and we did it all – from spiritual lectures to video series, to refurbishing homes for the needy. One of the videos that we showed was a home video, smuggled out of Iraq, which revealed the terrible persecution of the Christians there.

It's been said that you can size up a person quickly by simply asking them what it is that they worship. I think it's even simpler than that. I think you can size up a person by asking them what it is that they think about during their morning shower.

And soon after viewing that video, in my morning shower, I started thinking a great deal about the plight of Christians in the Middle East.

Besides being part Irish, I am also part Lebanese in heritage, and before long, I was ignoring State Department warnings and tracking down long-lost relatives in Beirut.

To make a long story short, I eventually made several trips to Lebanon, bringing family members to visit and do volunteer work for brief stints in a Christian Palestinian refugee camp north of Beirut. When we noticed that the children there had no athletic facilities other than a dirt soccer field, we raised funds through our Church at home so they could buy a basketball hoop.

And then something surprising happened. We had donated a basketball hoop to the refugee camp. As in one. But sometime later, when I asked the camp if they wanted a second hoop, they said there was no need anymore.

Apparently, some major government donor had learned of (or seen) the children in the camp playing on our donated hoop, and had in turn donated an entire modern basketball facility, complete with lights. So the next time my son and I returned to the refugee camp, we were able to run a full basketball clinic. After that, we hired a year-round coach for them…and then another…

…which got me thinking a great deal not only about coincidence, but about the larger miracles that brighten and enliven the world, which are so often inspired by people of faith engaging in first small (and sometimes later, large) acts of kindness. And about how these faith-filled acts so often have come together to make a civilization better. As Robert Kennedy once told the people of South Africa, struggling to end apartheid:

It is from numberless diverse acts of courage and belief that human history is thus shaped. Each time a man stands up for an ideal, or acts to improve the lot of others, or strikes out against injustice, he sends forth a tiny ripple of hope, and crossing each other from a million different centers of energy and daring those ripples build a current which can sweep down the mightiest walls of oppression and resistance.

"If Athens shall appear great to you," said Pericles, "consider then that her glories were purchased by

valiant men, and by men who learned their duty."
That is the source of all greatness in all societies,
and it is the key to progress in our own time.

We give thanks for the ripples of Christian hope that have come together to create great progress in society.

At its core, that's what this book is about.

At its heart, as you can see from the title of each chapter, this book is simply a thank you note.

DAVID T. MALOOF

PROLOGUE

THE BEATITUDES ARE THE ANSWER

I like to tell my children that kindness is the answer, to which they are apt to ask, "The answer to what question?"

To this, I always respond, "The question is usually irrelevant; kindness is almost always the answer."

The same can be said of the Christian teaching known as the Beatitudes.[1]

In fact, when it comes to the Beatitudes, what we can accurately say is that: "The Beatitudes have always been the answer."

As you read on, you will note:

- Devotion to the Beatitudes (Blessed are the poor in spirit), increased the female percentage of the population by some 40%;

- Devotion to the Beatitudes (Blessed are the merciful), created the institutions of the hospital and nursing profession;

- Devotion to the Beatitudes (Blessed are those who hunger and thirst for righteousness), laid the groundwork for democracy and for mercy in the criminal justice system;

- Devotion to the Beatitudes (Blessed are the peacemakers), created the "Just War" doctrine, which, once adopted, largely ended Christian religious wars, and promoted human and civil rights;

- Devotion to the Beatitudes (Blessed are those who

---

[1]   If you are unfamiliar with the Beatitudes, they are set forth in Chapter 1.

hunger and thirst for righteousness), led the movement to abolish slavery;

- Studies have found that Christians, following the Beatitudes, on average, are 25% more charitable than the non-religious (Blessed are the poor in spirit); and

- The list goes on and on – as revealed in the chapters that follow.

How does the Christian today use the Beatitudes for inspiration in a world so often filled with dark, ugly news images from around the world and dystopian films? The same way that Orpheus saved the Argonauts during the quest for the Golden Fleece. To avoid the seductive voice of the Sirens seeking to lure him and his men near to dangerous shoals, Orpheus pulled out his lyre and sang an even more beautiful song. The Beatitudes are the more beautiful, more seductive song needed in the world today, to overcome the powerful lure of the selfish life, that we as Christians must learn to play.

Of course, there is another point of view. It is commonplace today to hear people say: "Religion isn't the solution, it's the problem."

Few would deny that, for better or worse, religion has had a major impact upon history. By way of background, one estimate is that 8.8 billion Christians have, at one time or another, lived on this earth, with 2.4 billion of them alive today. An estimated 70 million of them have been martyred throughout history, and a 2014 Pew study, "Religious Hostilities Reach Six-Year High," found that

Christians were the most oppressed religion in the world, with some form of persecution in 110 countries. Incredibly, it has been estimated that underground Christian churches – those hiding from persecution, but maintaining their faith – would be the world's fifth largest religion if separately denominated. As Albert Schweitzer once said, with perhaps just a touch of hyperbole:

One truth stands firm. All that happens in world history rests on something spiritual. If the spiritual is strong, it creates world history. If the spiritual is weak, it suffers world history.

Still, there is plenty of ammunition to support the narrative that 'religion is the problem' – not just in polemics like Christopher Hitchens' god is Not Great: How Religion Poisons Everything (2007), Richard Dawkins' The God Delusion (2006) and Sam Harris' The End of Faith – Religion, Terror and the Future of Reason (2004), but also in academic works like Steven Pinker's The Better Angels of Our Nature: Why Violence Has Declined (2011).

Such opinions have gained support in mainstream society, most recently in reaction to the Academy Award winning film "Spotlight," documenting the Catholic Church's frequent mishandling of sexual abuse allegations.

Dawkins' God Delusion may be the most scholarly

of the "atheistic apologetics" genre; he cites, for example, to some actual social science research. That research takes the form of an esoteric sounding article purportedly concerning the correlation between social health and religiosity, by Gregory S. Paul, entitled "Cross-National Correlations of Quantifiable Societal Health with Popular Religiosity and Secularism in the Prosperous Democracies," *Journal of Religion & Society* (2005). Dawkins cites to this study of seventeen countries for his conclusion that:

...higher rates of belief in and worship of a creator correlate with higher rates of homicide...

In short, he implies that Western religious beliefs as a whole cause higher rates of murder. However, if you look up the study for yourself, you will see that the primary hyper-religious country that skews the homicide results is the United States. And if you delve further, you will learn that the truly scholarly studies that have actually looked into why the United States has high homicide rates never correlate it in any manner with religion, but rather focus on the lax gun laws, and other socio-economic factors. *See* Arkadi Gerney, Chelsea Parsons and Charles Posner, "America Under the Gun: A 50-State Analysis of Gun Violence and Its Link to Weak State Gun Laws," *Center For American Progress* (2013). A real study on the global causes of high homicide rates, the United Nations Office on Drugs and Crime (UNODC) "Global Study on Homicide" (2011), found that "higher levels of homicide are associated with low human and economic development," not religion.

More academically influential may be the opinion of Steven Pinker, a Harvard Professor of Psychology, and an atheist, who provides the opinion in <u>The Better Angels of Our Nature</u> (a book given to my daughter as required reading in one of her university classes) that Christianity has played no role at all in the steady decline of violence throughout history. As he puts it: "...to say that Christianity has, overall, been a force for peace in history is factually inaccurate." Rather, Pinker attributes the long-term trend toward fewer wars to factors such as the rise of the strong nation state and the growth of commerce and free trade – without delving deeper and recognizing, as we will discuss later, Christianity's contributions to a number of the building blocks (such as the development of constitutional government, independent legal systems, the Enlightenment and capitalism), which laid the foundation for these developments. As another example, Pinker attributes what he calls the "Long Peace" between 1945 and 2016, without a world war, to the rise of liberal principles in the dual form of the pacifying effects of democracy and capitalism. He further attributes "measurable and substantial declines in many categories of violence" to a series of "rights revolutions" including civil rights, women's rights, children's rights (and the decline of infanticide), gay rights and animal rights; ignoring, again,

Christianity's role in those developments as well. As for Christianity, he utterly dismisses it, calling it a religion that is at its core "benevolent hypocrisy."

Parts of the Catholic Church's history make it easy to dismiss. That history includes the Crusades (although attacks on Christian institutions preceded and arguably precipitated it); the Inquisition; the selling of indulgences; a long, sad history of anti-Semitism[2]; more recently, as mentioned, the Catholic Church's sex abuse scandal; and even to this day – again in the Catholic Church, the struggle of women to have their voices heard.[3]

Thus, as explained by Philip Jenkins in The Lost History of Christianity (2009), in everyday discourse, it is commonplace today to recite the Faith's institutional failures, and little else:

Whatever the religious beliefs of a given audience, a majority of people, whether in private or public life, feels comfortable referring to aspects of that history, and particularly to great institutions or events, like the Crusades, the Inquisition, or the persecution of witches. Media accounts regularly draw on a standard body of assumptions and beliefs about Christian history, which is seen as a barely relieved saga

---

2   A detailed summary of Christian anti-Semitism over the centuries can be found in James Carroll's Constantine's Sword: The Church and the Jews, a History (2001).

3   Of course, historically, secular regimes in the Soviet Union, China, Nazi Germany, North Korea, Vietnam and Cambodia have produced worse civil rights violations and a rogue's gallery of atrocities far more gruesome.

of intolerance and obscurantism.

And yet, Jenkins' research found such now standard discourse incomplete:

The conventionally negative account of Christian history includes much that is true, in some places and at some times: we need not look far to find religious hatred and anti-Semitism, militarism and corruption. But the story is much more diverse than is commonly believed.

Indeed, historically, the overall positive, civilizing role of Christianity was unquestioned. Consider this quote from T.S. Eliot:

It is in Christianity that our arts have developed; it is in Christianity that the laws of Europe – until recently – have been rooted. It is against a background of Christianity that all of our thought has significance. An individual European may not believe that the Christian faith is true, and yet what he says, and makes, and does will all spring out of his heritage of Christian culture and depend upon that culture for its meaning ... I do not believe the culture of Europe could survive the complete disappearance of the Christian faith. And I am convinced of that, not merely because I am a Christian myself, but as a student of social biology. If Christianity goes, the whole culture goes.

-T.S. ELIOT, CHRISTIANITY AND CULTURE (1960).

The renowned Depression-era sermonist Emmett Fox put it another way:

Jesus Christ is easily the most important figure that has ever appeared in the history of mankind. It makes no difference how you may regard him, you will have to concede that. This is true whether you choose to call him God or man; and if man, whether you choose to consider him as the world's greatest Prophet and Teacher, or merely as a well-intentioned fanatic who came to grief, and failure, and ruin, after a short and stormy public career. However you regard him, the fact will remain that the life and death of Jesus, and the teachings attributed to him have influenced the course of human history more than those of any other man who has ever lived...

To have been the religious inspiration of the whole European race throughout the two millenniums during which that race has dominated and molded, the destinies of the entire world, culturally and socially, as well as politically, and through the period in which the whole of the earth's surface was finally discovered and occupied, and in its broad outlines shaped by civilization; this alone entitles him to the premier position in world importance.

- EMMET FOX, THE SERMON ON THE MOUNT: THE KEY TO SUCCESS IN LIFE (1934).

Who is correct then? How, in just a few decades, could the entire verdict of Christian history have changed so dramatically?

And why enter this heated debate now with a book provocatively entitled Christianity Matters?

Daniel Patrick Moynihan, of course, famously chastised that "Everyone is entitled to his own opinion but not to his facts." The larger issue here, then, is what are the historical facts? And does this new anti-Christian scholarship represent its own new form of prejudice, resulting in a dismissal of the historical impact of two millennia of literally up to two billion individuals simultaneously, but independently, practicing uniquely unconditional Christian love? In short, are these critics effectively historical 'Christian love deniers?'

Jenkins, in another of his books, The New Anti-Catholicism: The Last Acceptable Prejudice (2003), lays some groundwork for such a thesis. Indeed, as we will discover later, when one digs deeper below the surface, both the spread of democratic theory and the very rights revolutions that Pinker opines as being causative of creating modern peace appear to be, in fact, at least partially, if not substantially, the result of the tiny ripples of hope propelled forth by the acts of a small number of committed Christians, followed by uncounted millions slowly but steadily joining in.

Could it be, as Eliot and Fox imply, that the beneficial influence of the various layers of Christianity, in many cases not through the formal church leadership, but rather through the inspiration of devout lay believers, has been so pervasive that, like the air we breathe, the roof over our heads, and the blankets that cover us at night, it protects us even while being largely taken for granted? Read on. Draw your own conclusions.

Four prefatory comments: First, no doubt other religions and philosophies also 'matter,' and deserve their own 'thank you notes.' The writing of this one to Christianity is in no respect meant to suggest that other religions may deserve any less. Consider for example, Judaism, and its promulgation of the still societal ordering rules known as the Ten Commandments. (Quite a debt is owed for that innovation alone).

Second, given its brevity, this book necessarily lacks the nuance of a scholarly book. For individual issues, I rely heavily on (am grateful for) and have accepted as fundamentally accurate the published work of others, most of it publicly available. I have tried to locate respected scholarship, but for better or worse, I leave it to the real scholars to delve deeper into these vignettes from history to mine the nuances.

Third, the reader may note that I describe a number of the subjects of this book as devout Christians, without referencing their denomination. That is intentional, because I prefer the reader to focus on the history of Christian inspiration as a unitary force, rather than upon the distinctions found in what one scholar has estimated is its 33,000 historically separate denominations. We diverse Christians certainly have far, far more in common than we realize. As just one example, the vast majority of Christian denominations recite "The Lord's Prayer." That is why it was so poignant, and natural, on September 11, 2001, that the passengers who spontaneously gathered in the rear of American Airlines Flight 93 recited that prayer in unison before they fought back and challenged its hijackers, preventing them from destroying the U.S. Capitol, and saving thousands of lives.

Finally, I am not a professional historian. I would love to receive any comments from such (or others) to improve the accuracy of this book. Nor am I a theologian. And yet I take some comfort in another Christian attorney, William Wilberforce, Esq.'s, simple explanation for why he felt qualified to write his spiritual book, <u>Real Christianity</u> (1797): "I would suggest that faith is everyone's business." To those who might reject the book as lacking as an analysis of the head, perhaps they can still accept it as a *cri de coeur* – a cry of the heart. To be clear, this is not meant to be a catalog, nor a full assessment of all of Christianity's historical successes and failures. Rather, this is more correctly seen as a kind of textual "highlight film" designed to record the successes, so as to inspire more of them.

Allow me then over the first thirteen chapters of this book to introduce you to those influential Christians (and others) who have lived according to the Beatitudes, to explore how the message of their lives, and of Christianity itself, has in fact resonated and evolved into larger historical trends, which impacted civilization through the centuries; keeping in mind that history is, in the end, nothing more than 'his [or her] story.' In the final two chapters, I will explore with you the theory and the evidence for why what I will characterize herein as true "Beatitudinal Christianity" is still today psychologically beneficial.

Herein then are the people and continuing trends that channeled the Beatitudes and sent some of the largest of Robert Kennedy's ripples of hope into our world.

—— CHAPTER 1 ——

THANK YOU FOR MANDATING EQUALITY OF DIGNITY FOR CHILDREN, AND ENDING FEMALE INFANTICIDE, STARTING IN THE 1ST CENTURY

(BLESSED ARE THE MERCIFUL)

❦

As my contact with real Christians, i.e., men living in fear of God, increased, I saw that the Sermon on the Mount was the whole of Christianity for him who wanted to live a Christian life.

-MAHATMA GANDHI

I t's commonplace today to say that all religions are the same – they all follow the Golden Rule: "Do unto others, as you would have them do unto you." And Christianity certainly follows that rule.

But, by its own terms, true Christianity, when it is followed as first preached, a preaching that we will refer to herein (in contrast to the many other paths that Christian teaching has since taken) as 'Beatitudinal Christianity,' goes radically further – it demands that its true followers treat others "better" than they treat themselves or that the majority of other people would ever reasonably be expected to treat them. Consider precisely what Jesus implored:

You have heard that it was said, 'Eye for eye, and tooth for tooth. But I tell you, do not resist an evil person. If anyone slaps you on the right cheek, turn to them the other cheek also. And if anyone wants to sue you and take your shirt, hand over your coat as well. If anyone forces you to go one mile, go with them two miles. Give to the one who asks you, and do not turn away from the one who wants to borrow from you. You have heard that it was said, 'Love your neighbor and hate your enemy.' But I tell you, love your enemies and pray for those who persecute you, that you may be children of your Father in heaven.

– MATTHEW 5:38-45

More specifically, as part of his famous "Sermon on the Mount," Jesus directed what specific values we need to put first, beyond just following the Golden Rule.:

Blessed are the poor in spirit,[4] for theirs is the kingdom of heaven.

Blessed are those who mourn, for they will be comforted.

Blessed are the meek,[5] for they will inherit the earth.

Blessed are those who hunger and thirst for righteousness, for they will be satisfied.

Blessed are the merciful, for they will be shown mercy.

Blessed are the pure in heart, for they will see God.

Blessed are the peacemakers, for they will be called children of God.

Blessed are those who are persecuted because of righteousness, for theirs is the kingdom of heaven.

- "THE BEATITUDES" – MATTHEW 5:3-10

This original Beatitudinal Christianity thus clearly presents a radical, idealized way of living; a requirement that we do unto others unselfish acts of sharing that we could never expect many of them to do unto us. This Be-

---

4   Scholars understand the term "poor in spirit" to apply to persons who empty themselves of the worship of material things so that God can fill them with a greater love of service.

5   The term "meek" in today's language has been interpreted as an admonition to be gentle rather than afraid. See Galations 5:23 (identifying gentleness as one of the positive fruits of the Spirit).

atitudinal Christianity is a set of "Golden-Golden" rules.

Following these principles, which were then fresh in the minds of Christians, Christianity in the first century actually brought with it an even more radical notion than the unconditional forgiveness of one's neighbor with which it is often credited. It brought into a tribal world the revolutionary notion that love and dignity were to be dispersed among all ages, sexes, ethnicities and economic status groups unconditionally. In short, the view, for the first time, that everyone is your neighbor. As one scholar has explained:

Christianity was to introduce the notion that humanity was fundamentally identical, that men were equal in dignity—an unprecedented idea at the time, and one to which our world owes its entire democratic inheritance.
-LUC FERRY, A BRIEF HISTORY OF THOUGHT (2011).

Thus, for example, Christianity established the doctrine (for the first time) that children had equal rights with adults. At the time of Jesus' birth, infanticide was legal in the Roman Empire. Children were considered property, much like slaves. Parents could injure them, starve them to death, trade them, or sexually abuse them. Christianity changed all that. As a result of this reversal of fortune, which Jesus inspired, it has been said by some scholars that it is hard to overstate the influences of Jesus' teachings on the fate of children. Thus, the following teaching of Jesus, which today seems so unexceptional, was in its day a subtle call for radical change:

Then were there brought unto him little children, ... and the disciples rebuked them. But Jesus said, "Suffer little children, and forbid them not, to come unto me: for of such is the kingdom of heaven."

– MATTHEW 19:13–1

Jesus Preaches the Sermon on the Mount
BY: JAMES TISSOT

None other than the Reverend Martin Luther King Jr. was inspired by what the early Christians accomplished in this regard, and he referenced it in his landmark April 19, 1963 "Letter from a Birmingham Jail" in response to those white ministers and others who accused his Civil Rights movement of demanding too much change, too fast:

There was a time when the church was very powerful—in the time when the early Christians rejoiced at being deemed worthy to suffer for what they believed. In those days the church was not merely a thermometer that recorded the ideas and principles of popular opinion; it was a thermostat that transformed the mores of society. Whenever the early Christians entered a town, the people in power became disturbed and immediately sought to convict the Christians for being "disturbers of the peace" and "outside agitators."' But the Christians pressed on, in the conviction that they were "a colony of heaven," called to obey God rather than man. Small in number, they were big in commitment. They were too God-intoxicated to be "astronomical-  *ly intimidated." By their effort and example they brought an end to such ancient evils as infanticide and gladiatorial contests.*

The remarkable, open-minded work of these early Christians thus laid the groundwork for today's widespread, worldwide Christian charity.

TODAY, BY ITSELF, CATHOLIC RELIEF SERVICES PROVIDES ON-GOING HUMANITARIAN SUPPORT TO AN ESTIMATED 100,000,000 PEOPLE IN NEARLY 100 COUNTRIES WITHOUT REGARD TO THEIR ETHNICITY OR RELIGIOUS BELIEFS. TODAY, ONE SINGLE CHRISTIAN NON-GOVERNMENTAL ORGANIZATION, WORLD VISION, ANNUALLY PROVIDES ONGOING FOOD, MEDICINE AND OTHER HUMANITARIAN SUPPORT TO AN ESTIMATED 120,000,000 CHILDREN IN 100 COUNTRIES.

❦

Christianity at its outset also radically improved the lives of women. To begin with, in at least three critical ways, Jesus himself modelled feminist ideology:

1) Jesus depended upon and received, in public, the ministry of single women. This would have been unusual in a time when women were expected to limit their public contact with unrelated men, and to perform most of their role in the privacy of their homes. An example of this is found in Luke 8:1-15, where Mary Magdalene, Joanna, Susanna and other women followed Jesus and ministered to his needs.

2) Jesus redefined the culture by receiving into his community women who were cultural outcasts, unquestioningly and without judgment. An example of this can be seen in Luke 7:36, where he interacts with a woman of ill repute. Other examples are at John 4:7-30, when he serves water to a Samaritan woman at the well, despite Samaritans being considered sub-human in the Jewish culture of the time, and, at John 8:1-11, his condemnation of those preparing to stone a woman for adultery, and his quick forgiveness of her.

3) Jesus broke convention by including women as teachers and disciples. An example of this can be seen in Luke 10:39, where Mary of Bethany sits as a full disciple at Jesus' feet.

Jesus and Samaritan woman at the well (John 4:7-30).

The fact that early Christianity (especially in the East) honored women should not be surprising, given that for the first four hundred years, the Aramaic Syriac Christian tradition was to refer to the Holy Spirit as feminine, using the Syriac word for Spirit, "Ruha." Indeed, as quoted by St. Jerome in his Commentary on Isaiah (On Isaiah 40.9), in the Gospel of the Hebrews, the Holy Spirit is seen as Christ's mother, who transports him to the mountain of his transfiguration. There, Christ is quoted as saying: "Even so did my mother, the Holy Spirit, take me by one of my hairs and carry me away on to the Great Mountain, Tabor." So even on a theological level, in the early Church, women were equally honored.

More recently, the mystic Thomas Merton explored and validated, as part of his own faith journey, the Eastern tradition of the holy spirit as a reflection of the divine feminine in his poem "Hagia Sophia." Merton's theology in this respect is wonderfully detailed in Christopher Pramuk's Sophia: The Hidden Christ of Thomas Merton (2009).

The early Church thus reflected Jesus' open-minded views toward women – who formed a large percentage of early converts. In fact, it was largely its attractiveness to women that caused Christianity to flourish (or in today's terms, to go viral) in the first place. Thus, in 370, the emperor Valentinian ordered that Christian missionaries cease home visits to pagan women. Too many were joining the Church – and one can understand why: women who became Christian found themselves better protected as both infants and widows. The early church scholar David Bentley Hart provides context:

> *Whether women of great privilege would have gained much by association with the Galilaeans can no doubt be debated, but there can be little question regarding the benefits that the new faith conferred upon ordinary women—women, that is, who were neither rich nor socially exalted—literally from birth to death. Christianity both forbade the ancient pagan practice of the exposure of unwanted infants—which is almost certainly to say, in the great majority of cases, girls—and insisted upon communal provision for the needs of widows—than whom no class of persons in ancient society was typically more disadvantaged or helpless. Not only did the church demand that females be allowed, no less than males, to live; it provided the means for them*

*to live out the full span of their lives with dignity
and material security.*

- DAVID BENTLEY HART, ATHEIST DELUSIONS: THE CHRIS-
TIAN REVOLUTION AND ITS FASHIONABLE ENEMIES (2009).

As part of this early gender rights revolution, Christianity thus brought with it the then startling notion (also
espoused previously in Judaism) that female infants were
to be treated equally with male infants. An entirely new
concept in a Roman culture, where, for example, female
infanticide during the first months of life was legal, rou-
tine, and widely practiced:

---

*Men greatly outnumbered women in the Greco-Ro-
man world. Dio Cassius, writing in about 200,
attributed the declining population of the empire
to the extreme shortage of females. In his classic
work on ancient and medieval populations, J.C.
Russell estimated that there were 131 males per
100 females in the city of Rome, and 140 males per
100 females in Italy, Asia Minor, and North Africa.
Russell noted in passing that sex ratios this extreme
can occur only when there is "some tampering with
human life." And tampering there was. Exposure of
unwanted female infants and deformed male infants
was legal, morally accepted, and widely practiced
by all social classes in the Greco-Roman world.
Lindsay reported that even in large families "more
than one daughter was practically never reared".*

The Children of Ancient Rome.

A study of inscriptions at Delphi made it possible to reconstruct six hundred families. Of these, only six had raised more than one daughter. (Citations omitted from original).

- RODNEY STARK, THE RISE OF CHRISTIANITY: A SOCIOLOGIST RECONSIDERS HISTORY (1996)

Christians, in their equal care for infants of both genders, thereby put into practice the simple Beatitude: "Blessed are the Merciful."

TODAY, INFANTICIDE IS ILLEGAL WORLDWIDE, AND THE WORLDWIDE RATIO OF MALES TO FEMALES IS 101 TO 100, ALMOST PERFECT BALANCE[6].

6   Unfortunately, the ratios remain out of balance in a relatively few countries with minority Christian populations. China and India remain countries where sex-selective infanticide or abortion still widely occurs – resulting in what has been referred to as "a hundred million missing daughters".

Women's rights under Christianity further improved in the sixth century, when the Christian Roman Emperor Justinian I managed to change Roman law so that he could marry a commoner, Theodora, who then became his co-ruler. Empress Theodora was a monophysite Christian, believing that Jesus had one nature both wholly divine and also human. This was in contrast to the Roman

Empress Theodora (c.500-548)

Church, which emphasized his two separate natures.

Theodora radically improved the status of women by improving divorce laws, allowing women to inherit property, caring for prostitutes and instituting harsh punishment for rape. Her reforms not only lasted for centuries, but more critically, they were gradually more broadly adopted throughout Europe. Today, Theodora is regarded as a saint in the Eastern Orthodox Church.

In summary, although the modern, institutional Church has been slow to publicly champion women's issues, the early Church did, in fact, play a leading role in promoting and advancing those rights.

—— CHAPTER 2 ——

THANK YOU FOR CREATING THE FIRST HOSPITALS AND DELIVERING THE FIRST OPEN ACCESS HEALTH CARE IN THE FIRST CENTURIES

(BLESSED ARE THE MERCIFUL)

Vincent Van Gogh painting of Jesus caring for the Samaritan on the road (Luke 10:25-37)

A new culture of courageous and sacrificial care for the ill – regardless of sex, status or tribe – was the second factor that caused the Christian Faith to grow rapidly.

By 'coincidence,' as a result of the Christian rejection of female infanticide, there suddenly existed in the Roman Empire, in the early centuries after Christ, an abundance of young Christian women available and predisposed to caring for the ill. And, even though life expectancy at the time was less than 35 years, during these years they, in turn, were both willing and available to care for those less fortunate with their health – to be 'merciful.' The result of that was the existence of a larger cadre of loving, nurturing women than had ever existed before, at this time in the Roman Empire.

In the third century, a massive smallpox epidemic hit. Pagans responded one way:

At the first onset of the disease [the smallpox Plague of Cyprian (250-266 A.D.), which saw 5,000 people dying in Rome alone each day], they pushed the sufferers away and fled from their dearest, throwing them into the roads before they were dead and treated unburied corpses as dirt, hoping thereby to avert the spread and contagion of the fatal disease; but do what they might, they found it difficult to escape.

- EUSEBIUS, ECCLESIASTICAL HISTORY, 7.22 (AS QUOTED IN 1965 ED.).

Christians, with their new, larger, female population, responded quite another way – unique in history. They did not abandon their afflicted, even those who were contagious. The inspirational quality of this loving, unprecedented conduct cannot be overstated. Soon, it was enormously popular to be a Christian. Bishop Dionysius offered this tribute to Christians' third century nursing efforts:

Most of our brother Christians showed unbounded love and loyalty, never sparing themselves and thinking only of one another. Heedless of danger, they took charge of the sick, attending to their every need and ministering to them in Christ, and with them departed this life serenely happy; for they were infected by others with the disease, drawing on themselves the sickness of their neighbors and cheerfully accepting their pains. Many, in nursing and curing others, transferred their death to themselves and died in their stead... The best of our brothers lost their lives in this manner, a number

*of presbyters, deacons, and laymen winning high
commendation so that death in this form, the result
of great piety and strong faith seems in every way
the equal of martyrdom.*

- EUSEBIUS, ECCLESIASTICAL HISTORY, SUPRA.

First Council of Nicaea — 325 A.D.

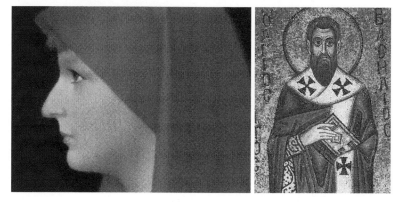

Saint Fabiola (Unknown-399)   *Saint Basil the Great (329-379)*

This Christian health care revolution was shortly
thereafter enacted into canon law, when the First Council

of Nicaea, the landmark meeting of bishops in 325, initiated the first widespread construction of hospitals anywhere in the world:

Before hospitals took care of the sick, the infirm were watched over by their family in their own home or they were expelled from the city. The earliest documented evidence of institutions specifically designed for the care of the sick was in the 4th Century B.C. by the Sri Lankans. The first teaching hospital was documented at the Academy of Gundishapur in the Persian Empire around A.D. 300-600. The expansion of the hospital system in Medieval Europe was driven in large part by Christianity. Before Christianity the Romans would care for each other as part of family-based obligations. The Greeks did the same. The First Council of Nicaea in 325 A.D. [organized by the Christian Roman Emperor, Constantine] ordered the construction of a hospital in every cathedral town in the Roman Empire to care for the poor, sick, widows, and strangers. They were staffed by religious orders and volunteers and were funded by the same.

- CASSANDRA PRICE, "HOSPITALS—A HISTORICAL PERSPECTIVE." CLEARLY CARING MAGAZINE SEPT/OCT 2007: 6-7.

Thus, following the mandate of the Council of Nicaea, it was Christians who set out and established the first network of hospitals in the world, starting in the fourth century.

One of the first to found a Christian hospital was Saint Fabiola, a Christian noblewoman of Roman descent. Her married life was miserable as the victim of a violent husband. She obtained a divorce and later even remarried (in violation of Church law). But her goodness was so profound that the Church took her back.

Fabiola's Christian beliefs led her to become an ascetic, renounce her wealth, and completely devote her life to the poor. She founded one of the first Christian public hospitals in the West, and personally attended to the needs of the sick, even when their diseases (such as leprosy) were as contagious as they were repulsive. Saint Jerome wrote of her as follows:

She was the first person to found a hospital, into which she might gather sufferers out of the streets, and where she might nurse the unfortunate victims of sickness and want...often did she carry on her own shoulders persons infected with jaundice or with filth. Often too did she wash away the matter discharged from wounds which others, even though men, could not bear to look at.

The Council of Nicaea's charge was also faithfully fulfilled by St. Basil in Caesarea in 369. The largest hospital complex in the Roman Empire called the Basiliad was founded by him, in part of what is today Israel. St. Basil's cavernous facility at Caesarea had over 300 beds, and separate hospices for the poor and aged. One author has described it in this manner:

[It] was often mentioned among the then wonders of the world, so numerous were the sick poor and so admirable was the care of them.

-ALFRED CHARLES GARRETT, MYTHS IN MEDICINE AND OLD-TIME DOCTORS (1884).

Thus, as the scholar David Bentley Hart has detailed, over the next thousand years, early Christianity's impact upon the care of the sick was most profound, with a single religious denomination eventually building over two thousand hospitals:

There was, after all, a long tradition of Christian monastic hospitals for the destitute and dying, going back to the days of Constantine and stretching from the Syrian and Byzantine East to the Western fringes of Christendom, a tradition that had no real precedent in pagan society (unless one counts, say, the valetudinaria used by the military to restore soldiers to fighting form). St. Ephraim the Syrian (A.D. c. 306-373), when the city of Edessa was ravaged by plague, established hospitals open to all who were afflicted.... St. Benedict of Nursia (A.D. c. 480-c. 547) opened a free infirmary at Monte Cassino and made care of the sick a paramount duty of his monks.... St. John Chrysostom (A.D. 347-407), while patriarch of Constantinople, used his influ-

ence to fund several such institutions in the city; and in the diakoniai of Constantinople, for centuries, many rich members of the laity labored to care for the poor and ill, bathing the sick, ministering to their needs, assisting them with alms. During the Middle Ages, the Benedictines alone were responsible for more than two thousand hospitals in Western Europe. The twelfth century was particularly remarkable in this regard, especially wherever the Knights of St. John—the Hospitallers—were active. At Montpellier, in 1145, for example, the great Hospital of the Holy Spirit was founded, soon becoming a center of medical training and, in 1221, of Montpellier's faculty of medicine. And, in addition to medical care, these hospitals provided food for the hungry, cared for widows and orphans, and distributed alms to all who came in need.

- HART, A<small>THEIST</small> D<small>ELUSIONS</small>, SUPRA.

As time went on, from the fourth century until roughly the thirteenth century, the vast majority of longer-term medical care in the Western and Middle Eastern world was thereafter more and more frequently organized in charitable Christian guesthouses, at monasteries and cathedrals, known as 'hospitium,' the precursor to today's term, 'hospitals.' Another author has described that development as follows:

As political freedom increased, so did Christian activity. The poor were fed and given free burial. Orphans and widows were protected and provided for. Elderly men and women, prisoners, sick slaves and other outcasts, especially the leprous, were cared for. These acts of generosity and compassion impressed many Roman writers and philosophers.

*   *   *   *

In the so-called Dark Ages (476-1000) rulers influenced by Christian principles encouraged building of hospitals. Charlemagne decreed that every cathedral should have a school, monastery and hospital attached. Members of the Benedictine Order dedicated themselves to the service of the seriously ill; to 'help them as would Christ'. Monastic hospitals were founded on this principle.

- ROSIE BEAL-PRESTON, "THE CHRISTIAN CONTRIBUTION TO MEDICINE," TRIPLE HELIX (2000).

TODAY, THE WORLD HEALTH ORGANIZATION ESTIMATES THAT THERE ARE 18,365 HOSPITALS OR HEALTH CARE FACILITIES WORLDWIDE IN 174 COUNTRIES

In the sixth century, the Rule of Saint Benedict, as it was known, was drafted and made to apply in every European monastic hospital. As noted in the quotation above, the Rules (which were followed for the next fifteen centuries) ensured that: "every arriving guest must be welcomed as if he were Christ" and that "before all things and above all things, care must be taken of the sick...". By the early Middle Ages, as monasteries added to their operating rules still other principles set forth by Augustine of Hippo in the fourth century, the result was society's first significant safety net:

Charity care was made compulsory for abbeys and it was every bishop's duty to maintain a hospice for the poor and travelers. The revival of Augustinian precepts encouraged incorporation of social work into religious practice. One medieval hospital records serving "the poor, pilgrims, transients, pregnant women, abandoned children, the halt and the lame- in fact, everyone." No longer just a refuge for the indigent sick and travelers, the hospital had become a bulwark against the tides of social dislocation.

- ERIC DARTON, "THE EVOLUTION OF THE MISSION AND DESIGN OF THE HOSPITAL." COMMISSIONED BY METROPOLIS MAGAZINE (1996).

The hospital, the world's first open source healthcare system, had arrived. Now all that was needed was a way to professionally staff it. That would happen centuries later – and it would be a singular devout Christian who would be responsible.

> TODAY, THE CATHOLIC CHURCH MANAGES APPROXIMATE-LY 25% OF THE HEALTHCARE FACILITIES IN THE WORLD, THROUGH 117,000 HOSPITALS AND 18,000 PHARMACIES.
>
> -SUSAN HAYWARD AND KATHERINE MARSHALL, EDS., WOMEN, RELIGION, AND PEACEBUILDING: ILLUMINATING THE UNSEEN (2015).

In today's world, it's hard to imagine a time without professional nurses, but it long existed. And it was one woman's destiny to prove the efficacy of and to establish this blessed profession.

Born to wealth in Britain (her mother complained that their house had only 15 bedrooms), Florence Nightingale believed that God spoke to her and called her to service while in her garden at the age of 17. Thereafter, she felt suffocated by both the trappings and the social niceties of her upbringing. She felt even more trapped by the contemporary requirements of being a wife—and so did not partake.

When the Crimean War broke out in 1853, the British public was shocked by the casualties, vividly reported for the first time in a more modern press. In 1855, Florence Nightingale led a troop of 38 young women (24 of them nuns) to the site of the battlefield. Initially stunned by the lack of facilities, the dirt, and even the rats, their first jobs were just cleaning the hospital.

Florence Nightingale (1820-1910)

But the military brass was soon convinced, perhaps by necessity, to allow her and her colleagues to assist the overwhelmed physicians. And what a dynamic assist she gave. Florence Nightingale was a health care force to be reckoned with. She not only cared for the ill, she developed detailed organizational rules as to how best to do it. One later study of the Crimean War concluded that using Nightingale's methods, the mortality rate among injured troops fell almost immediately from 52 percent to 20 percent. And so nursing as a profession was born.

Nightingale went on to found training schools for nurses and to record the details of her nursing methods in a systematic form – a system so logical that it is still referred to today:

Modern nursing derives so completely from the example and teaching of Florence Nightingale that it is hard to pick out the particular practices that owe their existence to her influence. All nursing has been influenced by her. One might say modern nursing is Miss Nightingale – that her name is a synonym for nursing. She demonstrated in a dramatic fashion in the Crimea that nursing – and sanitation – could reduce mortality.

*   *   *   *

Nursing literally did not exist except in a few religious orders until Miss Nightingale showed what it could do, and more important, established a school to produce people who could do it. The first school at St. Thomas' Hospital in London was a model for all later schools in England and the United States. Nightingale nurses became heads of all the early schools established in England. Bellevue Hospital School of Nursing in New York, the first in this country to introduce the Nightingale principles, was actually guided by letters from Miss Nightingale.

- MARGARET G. ARNSTEIN, "FLORENCE NIGHTINGALE'S INFLUENCE ON NURSING." BULL. N.Y. ACAD. MED. 32.7 (JULY 1956).

As of 2011, there were 19,200,000 nurses and midwives in the world. There are also presently some 746,814 nuns engaged in acts of service (many of them medical) worldwide.

Nuns were among the first group of women called to become nurses in large numbers, and over the centuries, they have been some of the most courageous nurses in the world. In the 19th century, the terribly deformative and highly contagious Hansen's disease, more commonly known as leprosy, was brought to Hawaii by foreigners. Starting in the 1860s, Hawaii quarantined an estimated 8,000 sufferers into the isolated Kalaupapa peninsula, to protect the population. However, that left no one to care for the lepers.

More than 50 religious congregations had already said no, when in 1883, King Kalakaua of Hawaii, in desperation, wrote to Sister Marianne Cope's congregation in the United States, asking her to take on the task. Sister Marianne and six other sisters said yes.

Sister Marianne Cope (1838-1918)

By answering "yes," these seven nuns had not only forswore material gain and committed themselves to care selflessly for others; they had also said yes to putting themselves at risk of being hopelessly and painfully deformed, with an incurable disease, in a faraway place, for hopelessly deformed people they had not even met.

Sister Marianne served on Kalaupapa for 35 years – from 1883 to 1918. Remarkably, she was never infected with leprosy. And, perhaps most remarkably, the leper colony was transformed by these heroic nuns, through God's Providence, into a place of joy. As written in The Atlantic in a retrospective article in 2015:

Many of Kalaupapa's memories are happy. Patients fell in love with and married each other; nearly 1,000 couples wed there between 1900 and 1930 alone, according to records compiled by the Kalaupapa Names Project. There were dances and musical performances, lei-making contests and softball games. Churches were popular gathering places, including one built by Father Damien, a canonized saint who contracted leprosy while living in Kalaupapa in the late 1800s. For many exiles, the Kalaupapa community—fellow patients, healthcare workers, clergy people—became their only family.

- ALIA WONG, "WHEN THE LAST PATIENT DIES." THE ATLANTIC. MAY 26, 2016.

In fact, it was Sister Marianne who personally treated the legendary Father (now Saint) Damien there, when he finally came down with leprosy. Father Damien is so venerated in Hawaii that his feast day (May 10) is a holy day of obligation there.

As of today, sixteen of the formerly exiled leprosy residents, aged 73 to 92, are still alive, and although the forced segregation was long ago resolved, six of them chose to still live on Kalaupapa.

For them, the area is sacred.

Committed servants like Sister Cope cared for those deeply afflicted by leprosy until, commencing in the 1940's, a medical treatment was invented. Today, there are only 200 leprosy cases per year in the United States; the disease has largely been eradicated.

⁂

Well into the 20th century, another disease remained even more widespread, and (seemingly) impossible to cure. Alcoholism. Until a devout Christian man took it on. Alcoholism was perceived for centuries as a moral failing, not a medical problem. In 1934, committed Christian, and then alcoholic, Bill Wilson was inspired not just to cure himself, but to heal millions.

In that year, by 'coincidence,' Wilson was visited by a drinking buddy who was then sober. Bill demanded his secret, which the friend revealed was his newfound belief that God would help him overcome his addiction. Bill explained that this would not work for him: he was not a member of an organized religion. His buddy retorted: "Why don't you choose your own conception of God?"

Alcoholics Anonymous Logo

Bill then understood that he, too, could cure his alcoholism and that "it was only a matter of being willing to believe in a power greater than myself." As he pondered that thought, still hospitalized for his alcoholism, he reported that a white light filled his room. In that moment, he said, he was a free man. He never took another drink. While he still lay in the hospital, the thought also came to him that there were countless hopeless alcoholics who needed to know the secret that had freed him.

Bill Wilson thus had a spiritual awakening through his belief in a higher power – and the realization that while he could not conquer his addiction alone, with God's help he could achieve total freedom from it.

In 1939, Wilson wrote his book <u>Alcoholics Anonymous</u>, to support his new organization. He and another alcoholic, Dr. Robert Smith, soon founded the organization by that name. While it does not work for everyone, using a twelve step program, which includes, as step six, each person praying "to whatever God we thought there was," millions of alcoholics have since used AA to defeat this once unbeatable disease.

AS OF 2010, 1.2 MILLION AMERICANS BELONGED TO ONE OF 55,000 AA MEETING GROUPS NATIONWIDE.

What leprosy was to earlier centuries, Ebola threatened to be to the 21ˢᵗ. Indeed, the contemporary story of Ebola, as it rampaged through West Africa, leaves us more thankful than ever for Christian courage. In 2014, the United States Center for Disease Control (CDC) predicted that 1.4 million people could be infected within two months – a number that would be exceedingly hard to reverse.

Dr. Anne Atai-Omoruto
(1956-2016)

Among the leaders in defeating Ebola were a committed Christian, Dr. Anne Atai-Omoruto of Uganda, plus three Christian Groups, Samaritan's Purse, Sudan Interior Mission (SIM), and the Catholic nuns of Liberia. They, working closely with more secular groups like the World Health Organization and Medecins Sans Frontieres (Doctors Without Borders) – although that, too, was co-founded by a devoted Christian, Max Recamier – led the way.

Liberia's health care system was in a state of collapse even before the outbreak; the country had only 50 doctors for 4.4 million people. After the outbreak, Redemption Hospital in Monrovia closed. In some areas, entire clinic staff were infected. After 300 health care workers had died, panic ensued – the diseased were afraid to visit the hospitals that remained open out of fear that they were contaminated. Foreign staff were withdrawn. The U.S. military flew in and set up 17 temporary treatment centers, but then immediately left to avoid possible exposure.

Yet, while even the military was on its way out, the Franciscan Sisters of Mary and their nurses were staying put and keeping the Catholic health clinics open. And Dr. Anne Atai-Omoruto was arriving. A Christian, family physician, public health specialist and mother of six in Uganda, in 2014 she led a team of 14 physicians to Liberia as a part of the World Health Organization's response. Together, they trained more than 1,000 Liberian health workers on how to manage the care of Ebola patients safely.

In all, an incredible 15 of Monrovia's 18 Catholic health care clinics heroically stayed open. Despite the risk. Despite the fear. Other faith-based groups, such as the aforementioned Samaritan's Purse and SIM, also refused to leave – fighting Ebola to its final eradication. As a result, the United States CDC turned out to be wrong – by over a million never to exist cases.

Estimates today are that only 27,000 people in West Africa ultimately contracted Ebola. The United States CDC simply hadn't counted on the courage and tenacity of the doctors, Catholic nuns and Christian missionaries of West Africa.

In 2014, *Time Magazine* named "The Ebola Fighters," its "Persons of the Year." In 2016, for her work in fighting Ebola, Dr. Atai received a special Global Five Star Doctor Award from the World Organization of Family Doctors.

In 2016, THE WORLD HEALTH ORGANIZATION DECLARED THE END OF THE EBOLA OUTBREAK IN THE THREE HARDEST HIT WEST AFRICAN NATIONS, LIBERIA, GUINEA, AND SIERRA LEONE. OVERALL, ACCORDING TO THE WORLD HEALTH ORGANIZATION, CHRISTIAN FAITH-BASED GROUPS DELIVER BETWEEN 30% AND 70% OF HEALTH CARE IN VARIOUS AFRICAN COUNTRIES.

In summary, Christianity has radically revolutionized health care in the world over many centuries, bringing it from a private affair to a service courageously provided, without discrimination or favor, to most of the world's population.

—— CHAPTER 3 ——

THANK YOU FOR BRINGING THE FIRST FORMAL EDUCATION TO THE MASSES, THROUGH THE CENTURIES

(BLESSED ARE THOSE WHO HUNGER AND THIRST FOR RIGHTEOUSNESS)

T he creation of the hospital in monasteries on the European continent was later followed, by 'coincidence,' by the expansion of those monasteries into the field of education. From at least the time of the First Holy Roman Emperor, Charlemagne (also known as Charles the Great or Charles I), who reigned from 800 to 814, monasteries acted as free schools (room and board in-

Emperor Charlemagne (c.742-814)

cluded) open to clerics, children of nobles, and youth. They covered not only classical education but also trades and craft, like stained glass production, and, of course, theology:

Charlemagne realized that his empire needed a body of educated people if it was to survive, and he turned to the Church as the only source of such education. He issued a decretal that every cathedral and monastery was to establish a school to provide a free education to every boy who had the intelligence and the perseverance to follow a demanding course of study. Since the aim was to create a large body of educated priests upon which both the empire and local communities could draw for leadership, girls were ignored.

St. Patrick (c.402-c.493)

- THE RISE OF THE UNIVERSITIES, FOUND AT HTTP://
WWW.VLIB.US/MEDIEVAL/LECTURES/UNIVERSITIES.HTML.

Early educational institutions also flourished in Ireland. The first formal Irish schools (to educate the clergy and nuns) began in the fifth century. This was thanks to two remarkable devoted Christian educators – Saint Patrick and Brigit of Kildare.

The story of Saint Patrick is filled with extraordinary anomalies. First of all, the patron saint of Ireland was not at all Irish. He was from the British Isle and was 'by coincidence' kidnapped by invading Irish pirates at the age of 16 and brought to Ireland, where for 6 years he lived as a slave working as a sheep herder. He prayed constantly for deliverance. Secondly, he is not actually to this day a saint at all; at least he has never been so recognized by the Vatican.

Many of the details of Saint Patrick's life are elusive. He begins his *Confessio*, or autobiography, as follows:

My name is Patrick. I am a sinner, a simple country person, and the least of all believers. I am looked down upon by many. My father was Calpornius. He was a deacon; his father was Potitus, a priest, who lived at Bannavem Taburniae. His home was near there, and that is where I was taken prisoner.

After escaping back to Britain, he studied in France, but eventually Patrick chose to return to Ireland as a missionary. And what a missionary he was. He became the

Monks at an early monastery school

first Bishop of Ireland and by tradition at least is credited with baptizing 120,000 Irishmen and founding 300 parishes, as well as hundreds of monasteries. He accomplished his goals by converting the clan chiefs first – and letting them then aid in the process. He wrote of no fewer than twelve dangers to his life, and numerous plots against him. Contrary to the myth, he did not drive the snakes out of Ireland, but he did drive out war, molding the warring tribes into one harmonious country, in the process ultimately converting some 90 percent of the population. Today, every year, on the last Sunday in July, some 40,000 people make an annual pilgrimage in honor of him 2,500 feet above Westport Bay in County Mayo, to Cragh Patrick, the location where he fasted and prayed for 40 days. The hand bell that he rang remains preserved in Ireland's National Museum.

More importantly, in the sixth through eighth centuries, the Irish monasteries that he created both accepted scholars from Europe and, along with Anglo-Saxon monasteries, sent out legions of devout missionaries who served to Christianize those areas that had never before been evangelized. After the fall of the Roman Empire, in 476, and during the so-called "Dark Ages" from roughly 500 A.D. to 1000 A.D., when Europe as a whole was no longer interested in Greek and Roman traditions, it was the Irish monasteries that preserved these teachings for posterity. This powerhouse of spiritual activity explains the title of Thomas Cahill's 1995 book, *How the Irish Saved Civilization.*

Similarly, Brigit of Kildare, with an initial group of seven companions, is credited with organizing the first communally-based educational institutions promoting consecrated religious life for women in Ireland. Her convent of Ardagh was the first convent to be established on Irish soil. It soon became a center of great activity, as many women, par-

Brigit of Kildare (c.453-c.524)

ticularly of noble birth, left their homes and flocked to the shelter of the convent. She went on to organize convents throughout Ireland, and to free many slaves. It is said that her charity to the poor knew no bounds. Because of Brigit, thousands of women came to receive an education in the Christian faith.

Said to be as beautiful as she was holy, Brigit, also known as Bride, is remembered as a model for women of all ages. It's from her nickname that the word "bride" came into general usage as the description of a woman getting married. St. Brigit is today the Irish patroness of poetry and learning.

In time, monastery education evolved into true high-

Pope Gregory VII (c.1015-1085)

er education. Pope Gregory VII brought that about. A man with a robust view of his own status – he declared that all Popes were by definition saints – he nonetheless managed to do something saintly. It was Pope Gregory VII who created the first widespread university system during the 11th century:

Pope Gregory VII ...was very important in the history of the university. In 1079, he issued a papal decree ordering all cathedrals and major monasteries to establish schools for the training of clergy. The result was a great expansion of education, with some places in which there were a number of monasteries concentrated, becoming centers of education.

- THE RISE OF THE UNIVERSITIES, FOUND AT HTTP://WWW. VLIB.US/MEDIEVAL/LECTURES/UNIVERSITIES.HTML.

The Christian monastery schools thus evolved into the first true universities in the Western world between the 11th and 14th centuries. They were modeled upon the great Al-Azhar school in Cairo, founded in approximately 970, and similar Islamic institutions, which taught, among other subjects, grammar, history, literature, astronomy, the Quran, Islamic laws and logic. But Islamic colleges such as Al-Azhar did not have the type of independent corporate structures that characterize the modern university, nor did they cover wide areas of learning such as medicine or the full classical liberal arts. Most non-Ilsamic subjects were not added until 1961. The curriculum at these new, largely independent, Christian universities, in contrast, covered law, theology, medicine, the natural sciences and philosophy, including Aristotle. These new universities thus had more intellectual freedom and covered a far wider range of subjects than the Islamic colleges. As they expanded, especially in the 14th through 16th centuries, they reached many of the masses.

Ultimately, Christianity went on to inspire the creation of many of the world's greatest educational institutions: the Universities of Bologna (1088) and of Paris (mid-11th century), Oxford (1096), and Cambridge (1209). By the time of the Reformation, in 1517, 55 of the 81 European universities had papal charters. In the United States, seven of the eight Ivy League universities had religious founders.

By the mid-eighteenth century, the Jesuits alone (with hundreds of high schools and colleges) had created among the largest single systems of education in the history of the world.

Thus, as with children's rights, women's rights, and health care, education worldwide was widely revolutionized by Christianity.

> TODAY, THE CATHOLIC CHURCH RUNS THE LARGEST NON-GOVERNMENTAL SCHOOL SYSTEM IN THE WORLD. BY ITSELF, IT RUNS 9,315 PRIMARY SCHOOLS, 42,234 SECONDARY SCHOOLS, AND 1,358 UNIVERSITIES.
>
> - SUSAN HAYWARD AND KATHLEEN MARSHALL EDS., WOMEN, RELIGION, AND PEACEBUILDING: ILLUMINATING THE UNSEEN (2015).

—— CHAPTER 4 ——

THANK YOU FOR INVENTING AND ESTABLISHING CONSTITUTIONAL GOVERNMENT, DEMOCRACY AND RELIGIOUS FREEDOM THROUGH THE CENTURIES

(BLESSED ARE THOSE WHO HUNGER AND THIRST FOR RIGHTEOUSNESS)

Despite being one of Christianity's fiercest critics in his day, Friedrich Nietzsche nonetheless recognized the role of Christianity in promoting equality of rights, thusly:

Stephen Langton (c.1150-1228)

Another Christian concept, no less crazy, has passed even more deeply into the tissue of modernity: the concept of the 'equality of souls before God.' This concept furnishes the prototype of all theories of equal rights...

- FRIEDRICH NIETZSCHE, THE WILL TO POWER (1901).

This chapter highlights some of the chief catalysts of that Christian equal rights revolution, beginning in the Middle Ages, and into modern times.

The *Magna Carta Libertatum* (*"Magna Carta"*) of 1215, latin for "the Great Charter of the Liberties," was the first declaration of governing principles ever forced by his subjects upon a Western King, and is widely credited as the bedrock document from which the fundamentals of constitutional government, based upon a balance of powers, evolved. It mandated limited power in the ruler and widespread political freedoms, including the then radical concept of religious freedom from state interference. For example, it prohibited arrest – even by a ruler, without the "lawful judgment of his peers or by the law of the land."

Christians, including Christian clergy, played a leading role in the *Magna Carta's* promulgation in 1215, and although it was annulled within just a few weeks by Pope Innocent, it was revived in 1225, most prominently through the work of the Archbishop of Canterbury, Stephen Langton.

Still others, such as the devout Oliver Cromwell (although ruthless in suppressing Catholic rebellion in Ireland), built upon the democratic principles laid out in the *Magna Carta*. Thus, in 1653, Cromwell refused the opportunity to be crowned King, instead ruling England under democratic principles. When the Monarchy was reinstated seven years later, it was henceforth (and is to this day) subservient to Parliament, setting this example as well for many future modern monarchs worldwide.

AS OF 2015, OVER 120 NATIONAL CONSTITUTIONS EXIST GLOBALLY THAT ESTABLISH THE RIGHT TO EQUALITY OF ITS CITIZENS, WITHOUT REQUIRING A PARTICULAR SET OF RELIGIOUS BELIEFS.

In the 17th century, building upon the *Magna Carta's* breakthroughs, modern theories of democracy were then promulgated, using Christian principles to posit that human freedom is a God-given right.

❦

Known as the 'Father of Modern Democracy', John Locke successfully argued for the first time that, in God's eyes, every free man had a divine, not a man-made right, to certain freedoms. They were, as he put it in his text Second Treatise of Government (1690): "Life, Health, Liberty or Possessions,". Locke, looking to renew Christianity, used it

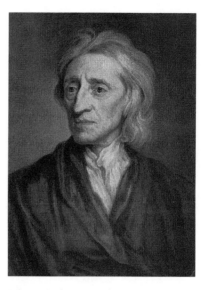

John Locke (1632-1704)

as the pillar upon which he built his democratic theories, deriving the fundamental concepts directly from biblical texts, including the Golden Rule (Matthew 7:12), the teachings of Jesus (e.g. his doctrine of charity, Matthew 19:19), and the letters of Paul, as well as from the Old Testament.

Locke was one of the principal inventors of modern democracy as a participatory system of governance. His concepts included more universal participation, political equality, majority rule, voluntary consent to be governed and individual freedom. Locke adopted the technique of

social contract to explain that legitimate political authority was derived from the consent of its people, and that
it could therefore be withdrawn if and when the freedom
of the individual was violated. Democracy, to Locke,
implies that the people are governed by their voluntary
consent. The power to govern vests in the people and it
is they, by their consent, who constitute the government.
According to Locke, the individual was naturally made
free by God, and thereby only became a political subject
out of free choice.

Locke also emphasized that all men are equal. There
was a perfect state of equality with all the power being
reciprocal. Locke, noting that the primary compulsion
to constitute a civil society was to protect and preserve
freedom, observed that society needed an established,
settled law; a neutral judge; and an executive power to
enforce decisions. He therefore foreshadowed later political works on the doctrine of separation of powers, by
insisting that the legislature and the executive had to be
independent of each other. Today, the principle of separation of powers, as was later expressed by Montesquieu,
is indeed one of the hallmarks of democracy and remains
fundamental for any democracy.

Locke noted that even after the establishment of the
political society, the individual retained a distinct and
robust private sphere. Also, as already noted, Locke espoused that man derived from the laws of nature the natural rights of life, liberty and property. He therefore emphasized that all individuals had these rights and that it
was the duty of the state to protect those rights, including

the fundamental right to own private property, because that too emanated from God and the laws of nature, and not the state.

Locke published a work entitled <u>The Reasonableness of Christianity, As Delivered in the Scriptures</u> (1695), in which he extolled the "Sermon on the Mount" and described it as Jesus teaching us "the laws of his kingdom, and what they [we] must do to be admitted into it." For Locke, Jesus was indeed the Messiah, but as set forth in the Beatitudes, he believed that it was Christ's moral mission which was primary, and that at its best, religion thus functioned as "a school of virtue." This work by Locke has thus been described as "a kind of unofficial lexicon of the Christian Enlightenment," establishing that reason and revelation could be rationalized with the "moral essentials" of the Christian faith.

Of course, the Greek Cleisthenes in 500 B.C. developed some of the basic concepts of democracy long before Locke, but in Greek society, active participation was limited to free men of Athenian birth – estimated at less than 20% of the population (Greek society was perhaps 40% slave). Locke also limited voting rights to landowners, but his underlying rationale, that natural rights come to all from God, ultimately led to a far greater broadening of the voting franchise.

A century later, as discussed below, some of Locke's most fundamental ideas were directly incorporated by Thomas Jefferson into the United States Declaration of Independence.

As of 2015, the freedoms that Locke deemed divinely granted rights are widely guaranteed. 144 out of 195 countries assessed by Freedom House are deemed either free or partly free, including 86% of Europe and 71% of the Americas, both Christian majority regions.

Unlike his more faith-driven counterpart and sometimes adversary, Alexander Hamilton, Thomas Jefferson had a complex relationship with Christianity, once writing to Ezra Stiles Ely that: "I am a sect by myself, as far as I know." Truly a maverick, he favored certain Deist concepts, then in vogue, which rejected standard Church structures and scriptural analysis, and he also denied that Jesus Christ was divine, yet extolled his teachings. As he explained:

To the corruptions of Christianity I am indeed opposed; but not to the genuine precepts of Jesus himself. I am a Christian, in the only sense he wished any one to be; sincerely attached to his doctrines, in preference to all others; ascribing to himself every human excellence; & believing he never claimed any other.

- LETTER FROM THOMAS JEFFERSON TO BENJAMIN RUSH, APRIL 21, 1803.

Thomas Jefferson (1743-1826)

Jefferson authored two books on Jesus Christ: <u>The Philosophy of Jesus</u> (1804) and <u>The Life and Morals of Jesus of Nazareth</u> (1820). Jefferson called the Sermon on the Mount (which, again, includes the Beatitudes):

[T]he most sublime and benevolent code of morals which has ever been offered to man.

More importantly, he relied directly upon Jesus' teachings in drafting the United States' Declaration of Independence. Thus, borrowing liberally from the Christian writings of John Locke, he penned that the rights of man came not from the government, but to men "endowed by their creator." He doubled-down on that by making the rights "inalienable." Thus, it was God who endowed mankind with rights. Governments were merely "instituted" among men primarily to protect those God-given rights. For Jefferson, the Bible, including Romans 13, was the direct source of this distinction.

Thomas Jefferson's genius in a wide variety of areas is not in doubt. There is a reason why President John F. Kennedy told a room full of Nobel Laureates, "I think this is the most extraordinary collection of talent, of human knowledge, that has ever been gathered together at the White House, with the possible exception of when Thomas Jefferson dined alone." As for his religious views, Jefferson, while again, not a believer in Jesus Christ as Lord and Savior, nonetheless promoted Christian teachings, and magnificently marshalled them to mold the guiding documents of a great, inspirational nation.

The author with Leymah Gbowee at a United Nations walk for women's equality in 2015.

In the 21st century, devout Christians continue to lead in promoting the development of democracy. Consider, for example, Leymah Gbowee, who fostered inter-religious cooperation to help democratize the African country of Liberia, which ultimately elected the first female leader on the African continent.

At 17, the raw brutality of the Liberian civil war with its child soldiers turned Gbowee, in her own words, "from a child into an adult in a matter of hours." Gbowee later married, and with five children to raise, became a victim of domestic abuse herself. Faced with a country in chaos and a violent home life, she turned to the Church for work. Operating out of St. Peter's Lutheran Church, her difficult job, as a social worker, was to rehabilitate former child soldiers. When yet a second Liberian civil war broke out, Gbowee did not sit idle; instead, she studied Christian peacemaking methods throughout history. Next, she bonded with other African women in a group called WANEP (West African Network for Peacebuilding) to try to end the bloodshed.

Gbowee says that she had a dream in which God told her: "Gather the women and pray for peace." Inspired by that dream, in 2002 she brought together Christians and Muslims under the slogan, "Does the bullet know Christian from Muslim?" Lining the streets, and dressed all in white, soon the women protestors' numbers reached into the thousands. The inter-religious group of women even went on a "sex strike," denying sex to their husbands unless they ceased fighting. The women eventually forced Liberia's ruthless then-President Charles Taylor to agree to formal peace talks to end the Civil War.

When the peace talks stalled, Leymah and some 200 women formed a human barricade to prevent Taylor's representatives and their rival rebel warlords from leaving. When security forces attempted to arrest her, she threatened to strip naked in front of them – an act that according to traditional tribal beliefs would have brought a curse upon the men. Leymah's threat was a decisive turning point in the peace process.

Within weeks, Taylor resigned the presidency and went into exile. He was eventually tried and convicted in 2012 as a war criminal, and sentenced to 50 years in prison. Liberia had found peace at last. And today Taylor is in prison in the United Kingdom.

Gbowee's success in overthrowing Charles Taylor and ending the Liberian civil war was profiled in a powerful 2008 documentary film produced by Abigail Disney, Walt Disney's grandniece, entitled: "Pray the Devil Back to Hell."

IN 2006, LIBERIA ELECTED ELLEN JOHNSON SIRLEAF, A CHRISTIAN, TO BE AFRICA'S FIRST ELECTED FEMALE HEAD OF STATE, A POSITION SHE STILL HOLDS AS OF THIS WRITING. GBOWEE AND SIRLEAF SHARED IN THE 2011 NOBEL PEACE PRIZE. TODAY, LIBERIA IS A PEACEFUL DEMOCRACY.

In the United States, committed Christian James Earl Carter has worked to bring democracy to much of the third world in the 20th and 21st centuries. First, he brought Egypt and Israel together in 1978 to sign a peace treaty as President of the United States. Then, upon leaving office, Jimmy Carter established the Carter Center in Atlanta, a not-for-profit organization that has overseen and helped to insure the integrity of 101 elections in 39 countries. Carter himself has traveled to 145 countries. To many, Jimmy Carter has completely re-invented the ideal of what a post-presidency career looks like. In 2002, he won the Nobel Peace Prize.

> TODAY, AMONG OTHER COUNTRIES, THE CARTER CENTER CLAIMS CREDIT FOR FURTHERING AVENUES TO PEACE IN ETHIOPIA, ERITREA, LIBERIA, SUDAN, SOUTH SUDAN, UGANDA, HAITI, BOSNIA AND HERZEGOVINA, AND THE MIDDLE EAST.

Perhaps President Carter's most powerful legacy may come from his 2014 book, A Call To Action: Women, Religion, Violence and Power. In that work, speaking as a renowned Christian, he demonstrated that his commitment to democracy and equality transcended gender. He attempted nothing less than to revolutionize the relationship between various Christian denominations and women, quoting Dr. Alison Boden, the Dean of Religious Life at Princeton:

The Gospel of Jesus Christ has at its center the ending of domination of every kind. For some Christians to use the Gospel to compromise the human rights of women and others borders on the obscene. Propagated with appeals to idealized heritage, immutable sacred history, and paternalistic care for the religiously ignorant, their rights-denying actions must be exposed for what they are – formal policies for the retention and augmenting of power by those men who already have it. The ethic of Jesus Christ proclaims the radical equality of human value. The ending of the subordination of women – and of all who are dominated – is critical to the building of the reign of God on earth as it is in heaven.

Every year, Jimmy Carter, along with his wife Rosalynn, also volunteers to build houses with Habitat for Humanity International, a Christian service group founded in 1976 by two other devout Christians, Millard and Linda Fuller.

SINCE ITS FOUNDING IN 1976, HABITAT FOR HUMANITY INTERNATIONAL HAS GROWN TO HAVE NATIONAL ORGANIZATIONS IN MORE THAN 70 COUNTRIES AND HAS PROVIDED DECENT, SAFE AND AFFORDABLE SHELTER FOR OVER 6,800,000 PEOPLE WORLDWIDE.

Leymah Gbowee and Jimmy Carter, as devout Christian leaders, thus follow in Christianity's long (although admittedly by no means entirely uniform) tradition of successfully promoting democracy and democratic principles.

James Earl Carter teaching a young boy to pray (1924–)

CHAPTER 5

NOTWITHSTANDING THE CHURCH'S OPPOSITION TO MANY ENLIGHTENMENT CONCEPTS, THANK YOU FOR ULTIMATELY RADICALLY REDUCING THE JUSTIFICATION FOR AND THE PRACTICE OF RELIGIOUS WAR, PARTLY THROUGH A PHILO-SOPHICAL EVOLUTION IN THE 5TH THROUGH 17TH CENTURIES KNOWN AS THE "CHRISTIAN ENLIGHTENMENT"

(BLESSED ARE THE PEACEMAKERS)

From roughly 1524 to 1648, brutal religious wars similar to those taking place today in parts of the Islamic world took place in Europe in Christian majority countries. That ended after massive casualties were suffered in the Thirty Years War, after more pluralistic Enlightenment concepts were accepted and after Christian 'Just War' theory ultimately came to be the dominant Christian theology.

Augustine of Hippo
(354-430)

Thomas Aquinas
(1225-1274)

Francisco De Vitoria
(c.1483-1546)

Francisco Suarez
(1548-1617)

While Cicero of Rome in the 1st century B.C. articulated an early just war theory, the first widespread acceptance of it followed Augustine of Hippo's comprehensive theological evaluation in *The City of God* (426) and Thomas Aquinas' refinement of that in the *Summa Theologica* (1485).

Aquinas ultimately defined 'Just Wars' as having three requirements:

- RIGHT AUTHORITY: Being undertaken by a proper state authority;
- JUST CAUSE: For a proper ethical reason and not for self-gain;
- RIGHT INTENTION: With peace as the ultimate goal.

Aquinas, who lived in a monastery from the age of five, had an influence upon civilization that went far beyond 'Just War theory'. Among many other intellectual contributions, his philosophy, called 'Thomism', set forth in his 61 volume *Summa Theologiae*, more often referred to as the *Summa Theologica*, integrated Aristotelian philosophy into Christian thought, and in fact demonstrated how Aristotle illustrated (if not proved) the 'truth' of Christianity's view of man having been made in God's image. Aquinas both identified and integrated into the Faith not only the four cardinal Christian virtues (prudence, temperance, justice and fortitude), but also the three theological ones (faith, hope and charity).

The reduction in wars has been tied to the intellectual acceptance of Enlightenment scholarship emphasizeing the rights of the individual between 1648 and 1789, including the further evolution in the same time frame of literary scholarship. There is no question that the Enlightenment ended a period of excessively doctrinaire religious thinking, which too often ceded political authority to the Church, and which was often cruel in practice. The Enlightenment thus radically altered the relationship between European society and Christianity. Some Enlightenment thinkers were atheists; others Deists – who, again, frequently viewed God outside of standard Church structures and scriptural analysis. Of course, it goes without saying that the Church opposed many, if not most, of the scientific breakthroughs and enlightment concepts put forth over the centuries.

However, on balance, scholars have also recently begun to accept the growth during this same time frame of the existence of a powerful parallel lay 'Christian Enlightenment' which actually served as a vehicle for progressive political and social ideas, i.e., put the Faith more in touch with the Beatitudes:

The political implications of the Christian Enlightenment are difficult to ascertain. It may very well be that it had a contradictory influence on political ideas and events. 'Reasonableness' and 'usefulness', toleration, reform and compassion for others: these were all positive, progressive, some might even say democratic, values that the Christian Enlightenment helped to disseminate. However, as mentioned earlier, Enlightened Christians could espouse very different political beliefs.... At the same time, however, they appear to have become more sensitive to social issues. Emphasizing the social rather than political benefits of religion, they increasingly stressed Jesus' charity, egalitarianism and benevolence towards the poor.

- CHAPTER 15, HELENA ROSENBLATT, "THE CHRISTIAN ENLIGHTENMENT," CONTAINED IN STEWART J. BROWN AND TIMOTHY TACKETT'S THE CAMBRIDGE HISTORY OF CHRISTIANITY: VOLUME 7: ENLIGHTENMENT, REAWAKENING AND REVOLUTION 1660-1815 (2006).

Indeed, it is worth noting that some of the leading Enlightenment scholars, including Francis Bacon, René Descartes and John Locke, were devoted Christians. Thus, their newly enlightened thought was, in fact, a form of enlightened Christianity. Also, since Christianity far outlasted Deism (which had peaked in popularity by the 1800s), it is this new softer form of Enlightenment Christianity, so to speak, that certainly has to be given a substantial amount of the credit for the peace revolution that ensued.

Moreover, the theological groundwork for this pacification of Christian Europe had already been laid over time. It began in 975, when the Bishop of Le Puy, France threatened the war mongering leaders who were instigating local violence, with excommunication. This then mushroomed, as other Bishops followed suit, into what became the powerful continent-wide 'Peace of God' movement, which effectively limited the "legitimate" days when warfare could and could not be engaged in. That was the first step toward reigning in warrior freedom on the continent.

Next came the popularization of the Just War doctrine. Commencing in the 14th century, Aquinas' principles were adopted and legitimized by the highly influential Italian School of Salamanca, which in turn popularized them among the European intelligentsia.

Later, in the 15th century, Spaniard Francisco de Vitoria wrote *Jus in Bello (On the Law of Wars)*, which revolutionized the law of war in three critical ways. Firstly, it effectively pioneered the rejection of mere religious differences as a just cause for war. Secondly, it condemned the killing of innocent civilians living among an enemy population, distinguishing seemingly opposing messages in the Old Testament. Lastly, it condemned the treatment of native populations in the Americas.

The next evolution in Christian peace writings came in the 16th century works of the Spanish Jesuit Francisco Suarez, including his *De Jure Belli (On Laws)*, and were considered so radical that they were prohibited in both France and in England. These bans, of course, greatly increased public interest in Suarez's works. His comments on Thomas Aquinas' *Summa Theologica* were so insightful that he was considered to be the most important theologian of the Counter-Reformation. He, too, rejected forced religious conversion as grounds for war; denied that Christians had any better basis to undertake war than non-Christians; and sought to reframe the justification of war as a matter of international law. Some scholars credit René Descartes, among others, with spearheading a 'humanitarian revolution,' in Europe. What is commonly ignored is that Descartes learned scholasticism in no small part from the Jesuit Suarez, and that he was also a devout French Catholic.

The 'Wars of Religion' in Europe from 1524 to 1648 demonstrate that Christianity did once permit, and even promote, violence, and no doubt, it was the massive casualties which led to the Peace of Westphalia in 1648 and the resultant European acceptance of the nation-state, which in turn resulted in greater religious tolerance and ushered in new, generally less bellicose, centuries. However, the long-term acceptance of such as the status quo—the failure to back slide—must also be seen, in at least some part, as the triumph of these new versions of Christian 'Just War' theory. This new theory no longer glorified wars of religious conquest, at least between Christian denominations, but rather sought to bond those denominations together:

The Treaties of Westphalia finally sealed the relinquishment by statesman of a noble and ancient concept...which had dominated the Middle Ages: that there existed among the baptized people of Europe a bond stronger than all their motives for wrangling—a spiritual bond, the concept of Christendom.

- HENRI DANIEL-ROPS, THE CHURCH IN THE SEVENTEENTH CENTURY (1965).

Steven Pinker in The Better Angels of Our Nature sets forth a chart which demonstrates that in Western Europe the number of wars declined through the centuries from roughly 2.25 wars per year in 1400 and less than 1.5 wars per year in 1500, to roughly 1.25 wars per year in 1850, to roughly 0.1 wars per year closer to 2000. Thus, in time, as these newer versions of Christian Just War theory became more fully ascendant, it, along with the 'Peace of God' movement, played a role as one of the pacifying forces in Christian Europe.

As THE ABOVE DATA DEMONSTRATES, AFTER THE NEW 'JUST WAR' SCHOLARS' WORKS HAD BEEN WIDELY DISSEMINATED, IN 16TH AND 17TH CENTURY EUROPE, THE FREQUENCY OF MAJOR WARS IN WESTERN EUROPE DE- CLINED SHARPLY, WITH THE MAJOR EXCEPTION BEING THE NAPOLEONIC WARS IN THE 19TH CENTURY. PUT ANOTHER WAY, AFTER THESE FOUR RELIGIOUS SCHOLARS' VIEWS ON JUST WAR WERE WIDELY ADOPTED BY CHRISTIAN AND GOVERNMENT LEADERS, WAR IN WESTERN EUROPE DECLINED BY WELL IN EXCESS OF 90%.

And through Christianity's influence starting in the 19th century, war itself, when it did occur, (usually) was far more humane.

Jean-Henri Dunant failed miserably at Geneva's College Calvin in all but one subject – he won the school prize in piety. He was also failing in business when, in 1859, he traveled to the Battle of Solferino, to seek the then Emperor Napoleon II's financial assistance. By 'coincidence,' he stumbled upon a battlefield where, after just sixteen hours of fighting between the French and Austrian armies, 36,000 men lay dead or wounded. The technology of kill-

Jean-Henri Dunant (1828-1910)

ing had evolved swiftly; the ability to care for the wounded had not. In this time, neither side cared a wit for the other side's wounded. Here is the description of what he found at the battle site, from his memoir, <u>A Memory of Solferino</u> (1862):

The stillness of the night was broken by groans, by stifled sighs of anguish and suffering. Heart-rending voices kept calling for help. ... When the sun came up ... bodies of men and horses covered the battlefield; ... The poor wounded men ... were ghastly pale and exhausted. ... Some, who had gaping wounds already beginning to show infection, were almost crazed with suffering. They begged to be put out of their misery. ... The lack of water was more and more cruelly felt; the ditches were drying up, and the soldiers had, for the most part, only polluted and brackish water ...

Dunant, on the spot, organized teams of women to distribute food and water for 3 days and nights; to wash vermin-covered bodies; to collect medical supplies and bandages; and to put a local church to use as a field hospital. He never did meet the Emperor, nor did he save his business. Instead, citing directly to the example of his predecessor Florence Nightingale, Dunant returned home to write his book advocating successfully for the creation of the Red Cross. He also drafted the original

Geneva Conventions on the treatment of prisoners, which ultimately led to the outlawing of the torture of such prisoners. He won the very first Nobel Peace Prize.

TODAY, THE INTERNATIONAL RED CROSS (KNOWN AS THE RED CRESCENT IN MUSLIM COUNTRIES) IS IN EVERY COUNTRY IN THE WORLD WITH SOME 17,000,000 VOLUNTEERS. IT PROVIDES ASSISTANCE AT AN ESTIMATED 70,000 EMERGENCIES (SUCH AS HOUSE FIRES) IN THE UNITED STATES ALONE EVERY YEAR, AND ON ITS OWN COLLECTS 40% OF U.S. BLOOD SUPPLIES. AS AN ORGANIZATION, IT HAS WON THE NOBEL PEACE PRIZE THREE TIMES.

While the first YMCA was founded in England in 1844 by George Williams, who was also a committed Christian, it was none other than Dunant who, in addition to establishing the Red Cross, also co-sponsored and co-created the World Alliance of YMCA's (Young Men's Christian Associations). In short, Henry Dunant played a leading role in the establishment of both the Red Cross and the YMCA as international institutions.

YOUNG MEN'S CHRISTIAN ASSOCIATIONS (YMCA'S) TODAY HAVE 45 MILLION MEMBERS IN 122 COUNTRIES.

More recently, we also need to acknowledge the work of Dag Hammarskjöld, a committed Christian, in

Dag Hammarskjöld (1905-1961)

fighting for peace and justice in the developing world in the 20th century.

The second United Nations Secretary not only forcefully advocated for peace worldwide, his revolutionary philosophy of sending peacekeeping troops into war zones, where that was supported by world consensus, is still being practiced today. In 1956, he made the hard decision to deploy UN forces to Egypt's Sinai area, and thus became the first UN leader to commission a United Nations Emergency Force to implement peacekeeping efforts. It has since been said of his UN leadership that he authored "the concept of peacekeeping as the world was to know it for decades to come."

Killed in a plane crash while on his way, under cover of night, to negotiate an urgent cease fire, he was also the first person to ever have been awarded the Nobel Peace Prize posthumously.

Discussing his faith, he said, "The longest journey is the journey inwards. Of him who has chosen his destiny. Who has started upon his quest for the source of his being." Of his accomplishments, he said, "I am the vessel. The draft is God's. And God is the thirsty one."

Steven Pinker's scholarly work <u>The Better Angels</u> perhaps pays the ultimate tribute to Dag Hammarskjöld, because it cites as a historical statistic that "the presence of peacekeepers [in war has] reduced the risk of recidi-vism into another war by 80 percent."

> OVER THE LAST 70 YEARS, THE UNITED NATIONS HAS FOL-LOWED DAG HAMMARSKJÖLD'S LEAD, AND HAS DISPATCHED EMERGENCY FORCES 57 SEPARATE TIMES THROUGHOUT THE WORLD TO ESTABLISH AND SECURE PEACE.

Contrary to popular perceptions, in terms of statistical risk, the world is indeed becoming safer. The research cited in The Better Angels further establishes that the odds of being killed by a violent act, such as in a war, (despite the rise in terrorism) today are infinitesimal compared to estimates that average 15% (and up to 60%) in the BC era. Pinker has also estimated in an interview that homicide rates have fallen from 30 to 100 per 100,000 in the 1200s to one and two per 100,000 in recent years. The work of Christians, especially the 'Christian Enlightenment,' and Christianity's promulgation and popularization of 'Just War' theory to much of the world, has to be given weight as one reason in recent centuries for the falling popularity of war, especially in Europe, as a means to resolve disputes.

—— CHAPTER 6 ——

THANK YOU FOR RE-COMMITTING SOCIETY TO THE CARE OF THE POOR, IN THE 19TH THROUGH 20TH CENTURIES

(BLESSED ARE THE POOR IN SPIRIT)

In the 19th century, the onset of the industrial revolution resulted in a large migration from the country to the cities. It also left masses of people unemployed, without food, homeless and destitute. Paris was a sea of slums.

At that time, a devout young Christian, Frederic Ozanam, was tested in a debate by an atheist:

You are right Ozanam when you speak of the past! In former times Christianity worked wonders, but what is it doing for mankind now? And you, who pride yourself on your Catholicity, what are you doing now for the poor? Show us your works.

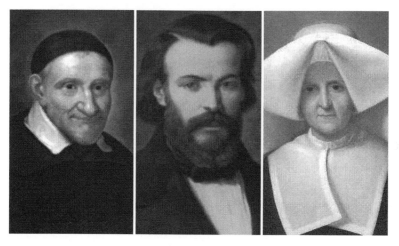

Vincent De Paul
(1581-1660)

Frederic Ozanam
(1813-1853)

Sister Rosalie Rendu
(1786-1856)

Taking this chastising as a challenge, Ozanam gathered his friends around him to decide what they could do to assist the poor. Saint Vincent de Paul was a Catholic priest whose extraordinary dedication to the poor and imprisoned centuries earlier (in the 16th century) was inspirational. Frederic and his roommate, in honor of Saint Vincent De Paul, thus began their good works first by giving firewood to a widow; and the Society of Saint Vincent De Paul was born.

Ozanam, in turn, took as his mentor a renowned Parisian nun, sister Rosalie Rendu of the Daughters of Charity, who was already running free clinics for the poor. In her spare time, she also ran an orphanage, and cared for the wounded during violent class warfare. With Sister Rendu's mentoring, the Society of Saint Vincent De Paul then flourished, and continues to do so, two centuries later.

TODAY, THE SOCIETY OF SAINT VINCENT DE PAUL HAS 800,000 CHRISTIAN LAY MEMBERS, IN 140 COUNTRIES WORLDSIDE, SERVING THE POOR AND DISADVANTAGED, INCLUDING THROUGH HOME VISITS. IN THE UNITED STATES ALONE, THE SOCIETY PERFORMED 11,600,000 HOURS OF VOLUNTEER SERVICE IN 2015.

Across the British channel, in London, William Booth was already a prominent evangelist. However, in 1878, distraught by the poor living conditions following the industrial revolution in the United Kingdom, he set out to go beyond mere preaching, and to assist the poor by creating a 'volunteer army'. His plan was to apply the Christian Gospel and a strong work ethic to abolish poverty, to house the homeless, to train new immigrants for work, to release prisoners, to care for 'fallen' women, and to aid the poor. His plans were so detailed that they included volunteer lawyers, bankers, industrial schools and even a seaside resort, all – and here's a twist on today's resort culture – exclusively for the poor.

William Booth (1829-1912)

As the Salvation Army grew, Booth earned the nickname "The Prophet of the Poor." When he died, 150,000 people attended his funeral. Yet another of today's Christian institutions of great charity was born.

TODAY, THE SALVATION ARMY HAS OVER 1,000,000 VOLUNTEERS AND 26,000 MEMBERS, AND SERVES THE POOR IN 127 COUNTRIES. AS JUST ONE EXAMPLE, WHEN HURRICANE KATRINA HIT THE UNITED STATES GULF COAST IN 2005, THE SALVATION ARMY MOVED IN ON AN EMERGENCY BASIS AND BY ITSELF SERVED SOME 14 MILLION MEALS TO MORE THAN 1.7 MILLION PEOPLE.

Closer in time, in the 20th century, Dorothy Day was a convert to Catholicism who dedicated her life to pacifism, social justice and women's suffrage. Her work spawned the Catholic Worker Movement, communities whose aim was to inspire others to mirror the life of Jesus Christ,

Dorothy Day (1897-1980)

dedicated to the care of the poor.

Day was born to a working-class Protestant family in 1897, and after being radicalized in college, participated in (and got arrested at) women's suffrage and anti-war protests.

A woman of refined taste, Day nonetheless chose to lead the vast majority of her life living in temporary housing, to wear hand-me-down clothes, and to eat soup kitchen food.

Her deeper spiritual awakening came in 1926 when, to her delight, she became pregnant with a daughter, after believing that a prior abortion had caused her to become barren. In 1933, she encountered one Peter Maurin, who himself modelled his teachings upon St. Francis of Assisi. After Maurin suggested that she publish a newspaper, with $57 that she had cobbled together, she rolled out *The Catholic Worker* – all eight pages of it – assembled in her kitchen. Within a year, she had 100,000 subscribers. As its editor from 1933 until 1980, she challenged Catholicism in her paper, as she put it, "by crying out unceasingly for the rights of the poor, of the workers, and of the destitute." Still today, it costs only a penny a copy.

Day and her followers lived lives of voluntary poverty, opposed war and championed civil rights and organized labor. In doing so, they befriended leaders such as Martin Luther King and Cesar Chavez. Day was feisty and street-smart, yet compassionate. One priest referred to her as "Mother Teresa with a past."

Day constantly insisted upon action: "The Gospel

takes away our right forever, to discriminate between the deserving and the undeserving poor." She judged herself by a tough standard: "I really only love God," she said, "as much as I love the person I love the least." And the Beatitudes were her Ten Commandments:

What are we trying to do? We are trying to get to heaven, all of us. We are trying to lead a good life. We are trying to talk about and write about the Sermon on the Mount, the Beatitudes, the social principles of the Church and it is most astounding, the things that happen when you start trying to live this way. To perform the works of mercy becomes a dangerous practice. Our Baltimore House was closed as a public nuisance because we took in Negroes as well as whites. The boys were arrested and thrown in jail over night and accused of running a disorderly house. The opposition to feeding the hungry and clothing the naked is unceasing. There is much talk of the worthy and the unworthy poor, the futility of such panaceas. And yet our Lord himself gave us these jobs to do...

- DOROTHY DAY, "LETTER ON HOSPICES." THE CATHOLIC WORKER, JAN. 1948, 2, 8.

Day fought capitalism's excesses, and even the Catholic Church, on its treatment of workers. When called in by an aide to Cardinal Spellman of New York and told to remove the word Catholic from the title of her newspaper; since it was not an authorized publication, she declined. Her argument was that, at the time, no one would confuse her Catholic positions with those of the Church. She opposed all war, including World War II. It has been reported that the FBI Director gave instructions that in the event of a national emergency, Dorothy Day was to be immediately arrested. Once she got arrested just for sitting on a park bench and refusing to take cover during a mandatory drill.

In 2013, the very Catholic Church that once battled her opened the case for her canonization as a saint. Then, in 2015, Pope Francis, in his speech to the U.S. Congress, singled her out as one of our greatest Americans.

TODAY, MORE THAN 213 CATHOLIC WORKER COMMU-NITIES CONTINUE TO THRIVE IN THE UNITED STATES, AS WELL AS IN 28 COMMUNITIES WORLDWIDE, ACTIVE DAY AND NIGHT, SERVING THE POOR.

You must already know of Albanian-born Mother Teresa (born Anjezë Gonxhe Bojaxhiu). On September 10, 1946, then an 'ordinary' five-foot-tall nun acting as the St. Mary school's principal in Calcutta (now Kolkata), she heard God's call while on her way by train to Darjeeling, India. The call was to work in Calcutta's brutal slums.

It was not a pretty place, nor an easy time. The Great Famine of 1942-1943 had claimed the lives of an estimated 3,000,000 to starvation in the Bengali province alone – and yet she followed that call regardless.

THE SIMPLE PATH
The fruit of silence is
PRAYER
The fruit of prayer is
LOVE
The fruit of love is
SERVICE
The fruit of service is
PEACE

-Mother Teresa's 'Business Card.'

Mother Teresa (1910-1997)

Mother Teresa ultimately led an order numbering some 4,500 nuns in 133 countries, including her own primary location in India, caring for the poorest of the poor, running hospices and homes for people with leprosy (over four million lepers treated even as of 1984) as well as soup kitchens, orphanages and schools. She famously once said that while it was popular to talk *about* the poor, it just wasn't popular to talk *to* them. She did much to change that. One of her rules was simply this: you give nothing to the poor, if you do not also give them a smile. She was a Nobel Peace Prize recipient (in 1979), and she did all this, we now know, from her private letters, despite her own sometimes profound doubts about the Faith. Posted on the wall in one of her homes for children was the following:

People are often unreasonable, irrational, and self-centered. Forgive them anyway.

If you are kind, people may accuse you of selfish, ulterior motives. Be kind anyway.

If you are successful, you will win some unfaithful friends and some genuine enemies. Succeed anyway.

If you are honest and sincere people may deceive you. Be honest and sincere anyway.

What you spend years creating, others could destroy overnight. Create anyway.

If you find serenity and happiness, some may be jealous. Be happy anyway.

The good you do today, will often be forgotten. Do good anyway.

Give the best you have, and it will never be enough. Give your best anyway.

In the final analysis, it is between you and God. It was never between you and them anyway.

In her later years, she had two final accomplishments: opening houses for AIDS sufferers and bringing her Missionaries of Charity to communist nations. Some recent publications have criticized the quality of the medical care provided by some of Mother Teresa's facilities, but even one of her harshest critics admits that while the level of health care that her hospices could provide was limited, at least, unlike most of the rest of the world, she did "something" for the underprivileged. When her canonization as Saint Teresa of Calcutta was announced on September 4, 2016, the people of Kolkata gathered by the hundreds in the streets to celebrate her.

There are many more Christian examples of commitment to the poor of course. Today, non-governmental organizations such as Catholic Relief Services (nearly 100 countries, as noted previously), World Vision (100 countries, as noted previously) and Save the Children (120 countries), founded upon explicitly Christian principles, combined with the more secular CARE (87 countries) and Oxfam International (90 countries) (which originated as a religious organization), play a central role worldwide. No one can dispute that they are part of the glue that holds this world together, or that, without them, the suffering would overwhelm our planet.

Devout Christians, following Jesus' mandate that the poor in spirit are always among the most blessed, have a long and proud historical record of serving the least resourced and most at risk in society.

—— CHAPTER 7 ——

THANK YOU FOR PROMOTING THE CONCEPT OF JUSTICE THROUGH THE CENTURIES

(BLESSED ARE THE MERCIFUL)

The Christian Roman Emperor Justinian I, during the 6th century, codified the Roman laws into the *Corpus Juris Civilis*, which is still the basis of civil law in most modern states. It included the doctrine of *"ei incumbit probatio qui dicit, non qui negat,"* or "Proof lies on him who asserts, not on him who denies," the first codification anywhere in the world of to-day's American concept of innocent until proven guilty.

Emperor Justinian (c.482-565)

In the 12th century, Pope Gregory VII rediscovered these Roman laws and ordered that from them a single continent-wide system of canon law, known as Gratian's *Decretum*, was to be created, an early system of universal religious law.

TODAY, THE DOCTRINE OF INNOCENT UNTIL PROVEN GUILTY, ADOPTED IN THE UNITED NATIONS "UNIVERSAL DECLARATION OF HUMAN RIGHTS," IS FOLLOWED IN NEARLY ALL WESTERN COUNTRIES.

Centuries later, in 1758, at only 30 years old, an obscure Oxford Professor, William Blackstone, having more or less failed in private practice, first assembled his systematic thoughts on the direction of the law for a class of his students. As they scrambled to take notes, lit-

Sir William Blackstone (1723-1780)

tle did they know that they were listening to one of the greatest recitations of legal principles in history. Famed philosopher Jeremy Bentham was one of Blackstone's students. Blackstone, he wrote, was a "formal, precise and affected lecturer – just what you would expect from the character of his writings: cold, reserved and wary."

A committed Christian, Blackstone had two older brothers who had become ministers, and he considered the study of law to be another type of Christian service. At the heart of Blackstone's thesis, like Locke's, was the theory that there exists a 'natural law' of rights which, relying upon the Bible, are derived directly from God Himself.

Blackstone's published lectures were an immediate success, selling out with their first printing, and being translated into French, German and Russian. In time, they would be restated in the Preamble to the Declaration of Independence, and shape the United States Constitution, among other documents. This is quite ironic, since Blackstone was appalled at the Colonies for their insurrection. His teachings ultimately laid the foundation for the law of the entire British Commonwealth - not to mention much of the world.

Of Blackstone's seminal work, his 1765 <u>Commentaries on the Law of England</u>, it has been said:

[A]ll of our [United States] formative documents – the Declaration of Independence, the Constitution, the Federalist Papers, and the seminal decisions of the Supreme Court under John Marshall—were drafted by attorneys steeped in Sir William Blackstone's Commentaries on the Laws of England. *So much was this the core that the* Commentaries *rank second daily to the Bible as a literary and intellectual influence on the history of American institutions.*

- WILLIAM BADER, SOME THOUGHTS ON BLACKSTONE, PRECEDENT AND ORIGINALISM. VERMONT LAW REVIEW 19.5 (1994-1995).

TODAY, 43 COUNTRIES IN THE WORLD HAVE A COMMON LAW SYSTEM, BASED UPON BLACKSTONE'S COMMENTARIES. IN RECENT YEARS, EVEN CHRISTIAN MINORITY COUNTRIES LIKE CHINA HAVE SOUGHT TO PARALLEL BLACKSTONE'S COMMON LAW LEGAL SYSTEM.

In the same era that Blackstone was creating the common law in England, a formidable Christian Italian intellect was about to revolutionize criminal justice.

Cesare Beccaria was an Italian lawyer and a Jesuit-trained Christian (if a rebellious and less traditional one) who joined with two friends to establish an intellectual group called 'The Academy of Fists.' In 1764, with

Cesare Beccaria (1738-1794)

the group's encouragement, and under a pseudonym, he wrote 'On Crimes and Punishments,' wherein he powerfully laid out, for the first time ever, the modern philosophical underpinnings for the end of punitive incarceration, torture and the death penalty.

At this time, since it was assumed that the afterlife would include corporal punishment for the sinful, torture in prisons was (believe it or not) considered to be beneficial – because it surely would reduce the quantum of suffering in the next life. Beccaria's group rejected this concept. For the sake of society's greater benefit, they posited, prison had to be geared neither toward punishment nor retribution, but instead primarily toward deterring future crimes.

An instant sensation, this thesis was considered radical, and the book was placed on the Papal Index of Forbidden Books. However, gradually, Beccaria's views held sway. Beccaria's work is still being relied upon today, both in the American and European penal systems, and he is considered to be the father of classical criminal justice system theory.

The legal and penal systems of much of the world today owe an extraordinary debt of gratitude to devout Christians like Blackstone and Beccaria.

FOLLOWING BECCARIA'S THEORIES, BRITAIN OUTLAWED TORTURE AT THE TURN OF THE 18TH CENTURY, AND BY 1805, MOST OF EUROPE, AS WELL AS THE UNITED STATES IN THE FORM OF THE EIGHTH AMENDMENT, BANNED "CRUEL AND UNUSUAL PUNISHMENT." IN 2007, THE UNITED NATIONS VOTED BY A VOTE OF 105 TO 54 TO ESTABLISH A MORATORIUM ON THE DEATH PENALTY. IT IS NOW VIRTUALLY ABOLISHED FOR CRIMES AGAINST CITIZENS IN 51 OUT OF 53 COUNTRIES IN EUROPE, AND IN THE UNITED STATES, ITS RATE OF APPLICATION HAS FALLEN FROM ROUGHLY 1 PER 100,000 IN 1700, TO ITS USE IN ONLY RARE CASES TODAY.

—— CHAPTER 8 ——

THANK YOU FOR REASSESSING, FIGHTING FOR AND REVOLUTIONIZ-ING HUMAN RIGHTS, CIVIL RIGHTS AND ANIMAL RIGHTS, IN THE 18TH THROUGH THE 20TH CENTURIES

(BLESSED ARE THE MERCIFUL)

Early Church leaders supported slavery, citing the Bible as a point of reference, and scholars like Saint Ambrose and Saint Augustine actually defended it. It was Saint Patrick who is credited (as a victim) as being the first moral voice condemning this practice, when he did so in the 5th century. It took John Locke's <u>Two Treatises on Government</u> (1690), es-

William Wilberforce (1759-1833)

tablishing the divine rights of man, and opposing slavery, to lay the philosophical groundwork to challenge it.

Building directly from and relying upon John Locke's writings centuries earlier on the natural God-given rights of man, in 1783 some 300 Quakers presented a petition with a radical demand to the British Parliament – a demand for the abolition of the slave trade. Those Quakers, along with a group of Anglicans with whom they collaborated, and who sat in Parliament (Quakers were banned from Parliament), shortly thereafter created the twelve person Committee for the Abolition of the Slave Trade, which included one William Wilberforce.

And what a force Wilberforce was! Elected to Parliament at the age of 21, from 1791 to 1834, Wilberforce led a relentless campaign both to reform Christianity, which he described as having become "servile, and base and mercenary" and subservient to "this perpetual hurry up of business," as well as to end slavery. He was right in one respect. British society at the time was, indeed, hopelessly dysfunctional, with rampant alcoholism – especially among the upper class – and a prostitution rate estimated by some to involve 25% of all of the single women in London.

Wilberforce pressed for Christians to reform their internal spiritual life along the lines of the Beatitudes. In his influential book <u>Real Christianity</u> (1797), his words mirrored the need to be simple in spirit. As he admonished: "Get going. Be useful, generous, modest and self-denying in your manner of life. Treat the lack of positive action on your part as sin."

To those who would not take merciful action to end the conditions under which slaves were traded, he detailed the precise manner in which the victims were chained together, suffered and often died, on slave ships. He then admonished: "You may choose to look the other way but you can never say again that you did not know." Wilberforce knew the trade well; one of his close friends was John Newton, the slave ship captain turned reformer who wrote the still poignant hymn "Amazing Grace." In 1807, Wilberforce succeeded in causing Britain to end their slave trade. In 1833, just three days before his death, he was advised that the British Parliament had gone even further and had taken the critical step toward passage of the Slavery Abolition Act.

Wilberforce's impact went far beyond just the reform of slavery. He also managed to change society's very mindset when it came to suffering. Before he began preaching, a person of lesser status was widely believed to deserve their plight due to an inherent sinfulness. Wilberforce succeeded in popularizing in British society the revolutionary view that God insists that the well-to-do improve the status of the poor, because their status is often the result of societal conditions beyond their control, and not necessarily predestined by God.

TODAY, WHILE FORCED LABOR RELATIONSHIPS STILL EXIST IN SOME COUNTRIES, CHATTEL SLAVERY OF THE TYPE FOUND IN THE 19TH CENTURY IS ILLEGAL IN EVERY COUNTRY IN THE WORLD. SLAVE TRADING WAS OUTLAWED IN THE BRITISH EMPIRE IN 1834. SLAVERY WAS OUTLAWED IN AMERICA WITH THE PASSAGE OF THE 13TH AMENDMENT IN 1865.

Actually, Wilberforce should be thanked once more. This is because his Christian faith led him not only to be history's leading advocate for the abolition of the slave trade, but also led him, along with an Irish Christian Colonel, Colonel Richard Martin, and a British clergyman, Reverend Arthur Broome, to establish the legal rights of animals to be treated without cruelty. Their advocacy led to the creation of the Royal Society for the Prevention of Cruelty to Animals, in 1824.

Wilberforce, Martin and Reverend Broome together established the RSPCA, the predecessor to the American Society for the Prevention of Cruelty to Animals.

TODAY, MOST OF THE MAJOR COUNTRIES IN EUROPE, NORTH AMERICA, AND ASIA HAVE OUTLAWED CRUELTY TO ANIMALS.

Sojourner Truth (c.1797-1883)

Sojourner Truth, born Isabella Baumfree, one of (an estimated) 12 children in her family in Ulster County, New York, took a most improbable journey to land on the back of the future United States ten-dollar bill, as was announced in 2016.

Daughter of a slave, and born into slavery, she was sold at auction, along with a flock of sheep, for $100. It was not a lucky transaction for her, as her new "master" was a violent owner. Then, to add insult to her injuries, she was sold twice more, in two years. Many of her children were taken from her and sold as slaves. She later sued for the return of her son, Peter, the first case ever won by a black woman against a white man in a United States court.

But good fortune did follow. New York emancipated its slaves in 1827. Sojourner, who had converted to Christianity, then became an itinerant minister. A brilliant woman, she traveled and preached widely, and dedicated her free years to the abolition of slavery nationwide.

Upon taking up her calling to preach the word of God, she changed her name to "Sojourner Truth," which seemed fitting for such an occupation. She wrote an autobiography, The Narrative of Sojourner Truth: A Northern Slave; as well as spoke out for abolition at the first National Women's Rights Convention, and then in 1851, gave her now famous "Ain't I a Woman?" speech.

Her range of intellectual and political interests was varied. A visionary, she moved beyond race issues, choosing to speak out for equality for all women (collaborating with Susan B. Anthony) and prison reform, and also to speak out against capital punishment – drawing large audiences. Before she died, she saw her abolitionist dream come true – thanks to the next gentleman.

Abraham Lincoln, the man who would issue the "Emancipation Proclamation," appears to have had a tumultuous relationship with his own faith. Raised at the knee of a devoutly Christian mother, he was unable to tolerate even a lie by omission. Thus, despite knowing that it would not be popular, he divulged in writing during one of his early political campaigns that he was not a Chris-

Abraham Lincoln (1809-1865)

tian, but rather a Deist (again, accepting God but not the divinity of Jesus Christ).

His faith appears to have begun to expand by 1862, after he lost his beloved 11-year-old son, William, and sought solace with Christian ministers. However, it was, in fact, the North's victory in the Civil War that appears to have finally led him back to Christianity. Remarkably, it was the very evening that he was shot – Good Friday, 1865 – during the play, that he turned to his wife Mary Todd in the balcony at Ford's Theatre and said:

We will not return immediately to Springfield. We will go abroad among strangers where I can rest....
We will visit the Holy Land and see those places hallowed by the footsteps of the Savior.

- STEPHEN MANSFIELD, <u>LINCOLN'S BATTLE WITH GOD</u> (2012).

The footsteps of the Savior? Arguably, only a believer would use such a phrase. But neither further elucidation of that thought, nor any such vacation, was to be.

Of course, Lincoln was long before that indisputably

an admirer of Christian concepts (such as the divine rights of men as explained by John Locke), in his messaging, as evidenced both when he discussed slavery, and then again in his first inaugural addresses:

I think that if anything can be proved by natural theology, it is that slavery is morally wrong. God gave man a mouth to receive bread, hands to feed it, and his hand has a right to carry bread to his mouth without controversy.

- SPEECH AT HARTFORD, CONN., ON MARCH 5, 1860.

Intelligence, patriotism, Christianity, and a firm reliance on Him, who has never yet forsaken this favored land, are still competent to adjust, in the best way, all our present difficulty.

- FIRST INAUGURAL ADDRESS, ON MARCH 4, 1861.

Indeed, Lincoln's short 701 word, six-minute, March 4, 1865 Second Inaugural Address is sometimes referred to as "Lincoln's Sermon on the Mount." It was delivered with victory imminent in the Civil War (and, as it turned out, just forty days before his assassination). In that remarkable speech, rather than castigating the South for the war, as his audience had expected, Lincoln shocked the nation by choosing phrases bathed in humility and forgiveness. He powerfully repeated this admonition from Jesus' Sermon on the Mount, found at Matthew 7:1-3: "Let us judge not, that we be not judged." He then ended with these words, now etched into the walls of the Lincoln Memorial:

With malice toward none, with charity for all, with firmness in the right as God gives us to see the right, let us strive on to finish the work we are in, to bind up the nation's wounds, to care for him who shall have borne the battle and for his widow and his orphan, to do all which may achieve and cherish a just and lasting peace among ourselves and with all nations.

In the audience that day was Frederick Douglass, the abolitionist leader. Later Lincoln, seeking affirmation, asked him what he thought of the speech. Douglass refused to even call it a speech. "That," he said, "was a sacred effort."

Also in the audience that day was a well-known 26-year-old actor, John Wilkes Booth, seething at the South's losses. Booth followed a different Christian theology – believing that slavery was God's way of favoring America. Ironically, less than two weeks after he assassinated Lincoln, when Booth was killed in a shootout, he had a Christian medal around his neck.

Moving on into the early 20th century, a single Christian missionary fought and ultimately succeeded in revolutionizing women's rights in India, the world's second most populous country, bringing an end to the thirteen centuries-long practice of child prostitution in Hindu temples.

Amy Carmichael (1867–1951)

Born to a wealthy family in Ireland, as a young girl, Amy Carmichael, along with her pastor, spent Saturday evenings handing out food to the local 'shawlies.' Shawlies were ladies too poor to afford a hat, so they covered their heads with shawls in winter. Young Amy assisted the pastor in securing enough funds to build the 'shawlie' families their own church.

Following that success, in the 1890s, Carmichael, still just in her twenties, moved to India to evangelize. By 1901, her focus had shifted to the care of orphans. One day, she delivered a stirring speech to a crowd, supporting the theology that Jesus did not believe in the caste system. Afterward, a seven-year-old Indian girl named Preena approached her. Preena had some story to tell: Preena's mother had traded her to live with, and to become a prostitute for, Hindu priests and wealthy donors – a fundraising practice that had begun in the 6th century.

Carmichael would have none of that. She told Preena that she could leave the temple and live with her. Indeed, she not only cared for young Preena, but she went on to work in India and to protect its youth for a further five decades. In time, she came to run 30 nurseries for young girls, many of whom had previously been forced into Temple prostitution. Despite being an outsider, she was determined to speak out, over and over and over again, and railed against the practice. Her 1905 book, <u>Things As They Are: Mission Work in Southern India</u>, was typical of her passionate exhortations:

> *But this I do know, and do mean, and I mean it with an intensity I know not how to express, that this custom of infant marriage and child marriage, whether to gods or men, is an infamous custom; that it holds possibilities of wrong, such unutterable wrong, that descriptive words concerning it can only "skirt the abyss," and that in the name of all that is just and all that is merciful it should be swept out of the land without a day's delay.*

In 1948, nearly half a century after she had first met Preena, in the wake of Carmichael's advocacy, the Hindu practice of Temple prostitution was outlawed in India.

TODAY, AMY CARMICHAEL'S FOUNDATION, THE DOHNA-VUR FELLOWSHIP, OPERATES A 400-ACRE COMPOUND THAT CONTINUES TO RUN AN ORPHANAGE, A HOSPITAL AND 16 NURSERIES IN INDIA. IT IS NOW LED BY INDIAN STAFF — WHO WERE PREVIOUSLY SAVED BY THE FOUNDATION AS CHILDREN.

During the same time frame, in America, it was Christian women who led the crusade to establish a woman's right to vote.

Frances Willard became the second President of the Women's Christian Temperance Union (WCTU) in 1879, and was a dynamic reformer who fought against domestic violence,

Frances Willard (1839-1898)

alcohol and tobacco use. She also fought for federal aid for education, free school lunches for impoverished children, unions, the eight-hour workday and strong anti-rape laws. When told by a co-worker that she had to slow down, and that her agenda was too ambitious, Willard rejected the advice flat out. Instead, she turned to what would become her movement's motto: "Do Everything."

In this time frame in America, rampant alcoholism and domestic abuse went hand-in-hand. In response, citing scripture's divine laws calling for equality, Willard and the WCTU pressed for women's suffrage, primarily as a means for women to eventually pass laws providing them with protection from domestic violence. Today, her movement might be called 'Wives' Lives Matter.'

Willard was a committed Christian, and, indeed, according to one study, 48 of the 51 leading women's suffrage leaders had Christian backgrounds.

The WCTU was, in its day, the largest and most influential women's political group in the United States, and in 1920, its lobbying lead directly to women obtaining the right to vote. The WCTU also succeeded in passing a constitutional amendment prohibiting the sale of alcohol, which was in effect from 1920 to 1933, in an attempt to stem alcoholism and family violence. Willard had succeeded.

> IN 1920, THE 19TH AMENDMENT WAS RATIFIED IN THE UNITED STATES, GRANTING WOMEN THE RIGHT TO VOTE. TODAY, EVERY COUNTRY IN THE WORLD THAT HAS VOTING RIGHTS GRANTS THOSE RIGHTS TO WOMEN, THE LAST ONE TO TAKE THIS STEP BEING SAUDI ARABIA IN 2015.

In the 20th century, although the Church failed to do enough to prevent the ultimate tragedy[7], there were in fact many Christians who made courageous, successful efforts to save Jews (and other victims) from Nazi atrocities.

Swiss Theologian Karl Barth has opined recently that while the Church certainly did not do enough, it did more

---

7   The nature of the Church's and Christian responses to the Holocaust is a complex subject, beyond the scope of this short book. The point here is simply that some individual Christians were heroic in that regard, even if the overall effort was deeply inadequate, and, even if it must be admitted that, sadly, many German Christian pastors during Hitler's reign actively supported the second class treatment of Jews if they did not convert to Christianity and did nothing to oppose their persecution.

than any other group to oppose Hitler. Similarly, none other than Albert Einstein paid this tribute to what the Church did:

Being a lover of freedom, when the [Nazi] revolution came, I looked to the universities to defend it, knowing that they had always boasted of their devotion to the cause of truth; but no, the universities were immediately silenced. Then I looked to the great editors of the newspapers, whose flaming editorials in days gone had proclaimed their love of freedom; but they, like the universities, were silenced in a few short weeks.

Only the Church stood squarely across the path of Hitler's campaign for suppressing the truth. I never had any special interest in the Church before, but now I feel a great affection and admiration for it because the Church alone has had the courage and persistence to stand for intellectual and moral freedom. I am forced to confess that what I once despised I now praise unreservedly.

- ALBERT EINSTEIN, AS QUOTED IN "TIME," DECEMBER 23, 1940.

Dietrich Bonhoeffer, author of The Cost of Discipleship (1937) was a German Lutheran pastor, theologian and anti-Nazi dissident, who immediately rejected an early Nazi order that the Old Testament be removed from

Dietrich Bonhoeffer (1906-1945)

bibles. Secretly, Bonhoeffer and his relatives also personally saved Jews from the 'final solution' by disguising them as German special agents, among several missions he was involved with to ferry Jews into Switzerland and England. He eventually became vocal in his opposition to Hitler and the Jewish genocide, and ultimately, he was complicit in a plot to kill the Fuhrer. He paid for that with commitment to two concentration camps, until he was eventually hanged by order of Hitler himself in 1945, just three weeks before the war ended.

Bonhoeffer's devotion to the principles in the Beatitudes was clear. In his book <u>Life Together</u> (1939), he set forth the ideal of what life in a community should be like. It includes a section on "The Ministry of Meekness," concerning which he explains, "He who would learn to serve, must first learn to think little of himself." The book references another necessary ministry for Christians: "The Ministry of Helpfulness," which involves doing small acts of service to others, rather than being solely focused on acts related to material gain ("Blessed are the poor in spirit"). It also includes a section on "The Ministry of Bearing" in which he refers to those who suffer the sins of others, but do not need to judge ("Blessed are those who are persecuted"). He requires that we forgive those with whom we live, and that we verbally do so on a daily basis. Bonhoeffer thus expressly both taught and lived the Beatitudes.

Martin Luther King acknowledged Bonhoeffer this way:

If your opponent has a conscience, then follow Gandhi and nonviolence. But if your enemy has no conscience like Hitler, then follow Bonhoeffer.

An estimated one third of German Catholic priests faced some form of reprisal from the Nazi government and 400 German priests were sent to the dedicated Priest Barracks of Dachau Concentration Camp alone.

Moreover, it was Christian pastors who succeeded in forcing Hitler to publicly end and ultimately to curtail his euthanasia initiative – known as the T4 Program – of killing the incurably ill, elderly and mentally or physically disabled.

In the Netherlands in 1941, Catholics organized a series of strikes and protests against the Nazi treatment of the Jews. In July 1942, the Nazis declared that all Jewish converts, or spouses of Christians, would be exempted from deportation if the opposition ceased. The Archbishop of Utrecht, Johannes de Jong, refused; while other churches agreed. In response, the authorities deported all Catholics of Jewish blood, including the future saint Edith Stein, while exempting 9,000 Protestant Jews. By the end of the war, Dutch Catholics had helped thousands of Jews to escape and hid another 40,000. Forty-nine Dutch priests gave their lives in this effort.

Similarly, in Bulgaria, both the Patriarch Konstantin (Cyril) Markov Konstantinov, and the Orthodox Church, through lay members such as Dimitar Peshev, successfully refused to aid the Nazis in collecting approximately 48,000 Jews.

In Denmark, King Christian X told the Nazis that if Jews were forced to wear a gold star, he would wear one too. The Danish Lutheran Church similarly refused all cooperation, and even read aloud in every church a letter of protest against the round-up of Jews on October 2, 1943, successfully saving an estimated 8,000 Jews.

Father Maximilian Kolbe (1894-1941)

In Poland, Father Maximilian Kolbe's Franciscan friary provided shelter to some 2,000 Jewish refugees. In 1941, Father Kolbe was arrested and taken to Auschwitz. After one of the inmates in his barracks went missing, the Nazis selected ten inmates to be starved to death, to deter future escapes. Because he had no children, Father Kolbe voluntarily traded places with one of the ten, a married man with a family. "I will take his place," Kolbe said, "I am alone. I am a Catholic priest." The man whose life Father Kolbe spared, Franciszek Gajowniczek, lived another 53 years, until 1995. Father Kolbe was canonized as Saint Maximilian Kolbe on October 10, 1982.

Overall, the computer database at Yad Vashem (Holocaust Museum) in Israel lists no less than 26,119 persons as being "The Righteous Among Nations," meaning that they were non-Jews actively involved in helping to rescue Jews during that event. The largest numbers were in Belgium, Poland, the Netherlands and France.

It is widely agreed that hundreds of thousands of Jews in Europe were saved through the efforts of the various Churches.

IN 1965, THE SECOND VATICAN COUNCIL ISSUED NOSTRA AETATE, A LANDMARK DOCUMENT CONDEMNING CHRISTIANITY'S HISTORY OF ANTI-SEMITISM. IT CALLED FOR ESTEEM FOR OTHER RELIGIONS, INCLUDING JEWS. IT PASSED BY A VOTE OF 2,221 TO 88. THESE VIEWS WERE REITERATED IN DECEMBER OF 2015, WHEN THE VATICAN ISSUED A THEOLOGICAL STATEMENT REJECTING WHOLESALE ATTEMPTS TO CONVERT JEWS TO CHRISTIANITY.

Eleanor Roosevelt prayed nearly every evening. She was a remarkable First Lady, who pushed her husband, President Franklin Roosevelt, to support federal 'anti-lynching' laws – although they never passed due to certain influential Southern legislators' opposition. Following the death of her husband, whose efforts led to the creation of the United Nations, she pressed for the United States to join it, and served as America's first Representative.

Later, Roosevelt chaired the U.N.'s first Human Rights Council. Her greatest accomplishment is believed to be in spearheading the drafting of the 1948 Universal Declaration of Human Rights, the world's first attempt to delineate common ethical standards for the treatment of all human beings.

Ms. Roosevelt was powerfully aided in her endeavor by a nexus of dedicated liberal Christian clerics and laity, inspired by the Edinburgh Missionary Conference of 1910. That Missionary Conference brought a variety of Protestant denominations together, primarily to promote missionary outreach, but in the process also undertook the first serious effort to reach the goal of establishing religious freedom worldwide.

Eleanor Roosevelt (1884-1962)

The Universal Declaration was followed by the International Bill of Human Rights, and in 1966, the UN

General Assembly adopted the entire International Bill of Human Rights. In 1976, because of ratifications by a sufficient number of individual nations, the International Bill of Rights, including Eleanor Roosevelt's Universal Declaration of Human Rights, took on the force of international law.

It was recently announced that Eleanor Roosevelt will be on the back of United States five dollar bills.

THE UNITED NATIONS HAS 193 MEMBER NATIONS. THE UNIVERSAL DECLARATION OF HUMAN RIGHTS HAS BEEN EXPLICITLY ADOPTED BY THE UN FOR THE PURPOSE OF DEFINING THE TERM "HUMAN RIGHTS" AS IT APPEARS IN THE UN CHARTER. THUS, TODAY, THAT UNIVERSAL DECLARATION IS BINDING UPON ALL 193 OF ITS UN MEMBER STATES.

In more recent years, Nelson Mandela and Bishop Desmond Tutu led the way to end Apartheid in South Africa. South Africa was ruled under racist policies commencing in 1795, and under structural apartheid laws after the election of 1948, both purported to be justified by Christian beliefs.

Nelson Mandela, born in 1918 to a mother who was a committed Christian, learned a different theology. His baptized name "Rolihlahla" means "troublemaker," and so he would become for the ruling class of South Africa. Sent to a Methodist Church School from the age of 7, he

Nelson Mandela (1918-2013)

attended its services every Sunday – and here is the life lesson that he walked away with:

> *The Church was as concerned with this world as the next: I saw that virtually all of the achievements of Africans seemed to have come about through the missionary work of the Church.*
>
> - NELSON MANDELA, LONG WALK TO FREEDOM (1994).

Mandela was so spiritually moved that he taught Bible classes as a college student.

As a young law student, he came to prominence as a result of joining the African National Congress (ANC).

In 1950, he was appointed head of the ANC Youth League. Inspired by Gandhi, he formed a "Defiance Committee" against apartheid, using nonviolent resistance and boycotts to press for race-neutral laws. Under his leadership, membership jumped from 10,000 to 100,000. In response, the government imposed martial law and embarked on mass arrests. Mandela himself was barred from meeting with more than one person at a time, and from speaking in public. He was frequently arrested.

Once admitted to the bar as a lawyer, he formed Mandela and Tambo, South Africa's first all-black law firm, specializing in cases of police brutality. Work was plentiful.

In 1962, when nonviolent resistance had clearly failed to make progress, Mandela's group eventually turned to violence, primarily targeting public properties.

However, starting in the mid-to-late 1980s, the struggle again became largely nonviolent, focused upon cultural, academic and athletic boycotts, both inside and outside of South Africa. These measures had a strong effect. Around the world, protests by Church groups, college students, labor unions and progressive organizations eventually led to most of the industrialized nations of the world instituting sanctions. At the same time, white majority and even law enforcement's support for the rulers in South Africa began to diminish when the movement's nonviolent protests were responded to with brutality.

Mandela was arrested and ultimately incarcerated for 27 years, with a large portion of that time being spent in the notorious Robben Island prison, until international pressure forced his release in 1990.

In the ultimate demonstration of his evolution towards nonviolence and Christian forgiveness, on the day of his release, he suddenly went missing -- because he was seeking to have tea with South Africa's last apartheid leader — F.W. de Klerk.

Miraculously, Mandela's formation of a new black majority government was largely peaceful, and without retribution toward the white minority by the new leaders. Mandela's ultimate adoption of peaceful co-existence extended beyond South Africa's white minority. He also played a leading role in reconciling two of South Africa's competing tribes, whose animus towards each other was deep-seated: the Zulus and the Xhosas.

Speaking of Christ, Mandela evoked the eighth Beatitude, describing him as the Messiah "whose life testifies to the truth that there is no shame in being oppressed. Those who should be ashamed are those who oppress others."

During what he later referred to as his "long holiday" in prison, Mandela avoided hate by focusing on the humanity of his jailers and by frequently repeating these lines from the British poet William Henley's 1888 poem *"Invictus"* (latin for 'unconquered'), a poem which was also a favorite of Franklin Roosevelt:

> *Out of the night that covers me,*
> *Black as the Pit from pole to pole,*
> *I thank whatever gods may be*
> *For my unconquerable soul.*
>
> *In the fell clutch of circumstance*
> *I have not winced nor cried aloud.*
> *Under the bludgeonings of chance*

My head is bloody, but unbowed.

Beyond this place of wrath and tears
Looms but the Horror of the shade,
And yet the menace of the years
Finds, and shall find, me unafraid.

It matters not how strait the gate,
How charged with punishments the scroll.
I am the master of my fate,
I am the captain of my soul.

Today, his massive, unconquerable statue stands out-side what were once the prison gates of Robben Island.

Mandela was chosen as the 1993 Nobel Peace Prize winner, a prize that he shared with former President de Klerk. He summarized his revolutionary inspiration suc-cinctly: "Religion was one of the motivating factors in everything we did." He went from prisoner to President and ended apartheid in 1994.

❦

Mandela's colleague and compatriot, Bishop Des-mond Tutu, won the Nobel Peace Prize in 1984. As with Mandela, his first religious inspiration came as a young man. Asked why he joined the clergy, he explained that his mother was a single woman, a cleaner and a cook at a school for the blind:

*One day...I was standing in the street with my
mother when a white man in a priest's clothing
walked past. As he passed us he took off his hat to
my mother. I couldn't believe my eyes—a white man
who greeted a black working class woman!*

- "THE NOBEL PEACE PRIZE 1984 – PRESENTATION
SPEECH." FOUND AT NOBELPRIZE.ORG.

Bishop Desmond Tutu (1931–)

By 'coincidence,' the man tipping his hat to the young Desmond Tutu's mother was none other than a monk named Trevor Huddleston, later an Anglican bishop, and in time one of apartheid's most tireless opponents. Huddleston, Tutu and a third cleric, an English Anglican priest named John Collins, a worldwide fundraiser against apartheid, formed a powerful clerical triumvirate, who joined with Mandela to not only eventually bring apartheid to its knees, but to ensure that real democracy followed that fully included the white minority. Bishop Tutu also headed a national "Truth and Reconciliation Commission" to ensure that real Christian forgiveness for those who had previously supported apartheid followed after the black population had its freedom.

'Working' may be the word that best summarizes Bishop Tutu's life. How he has worked, and worked, and worked:

- As the leading spiritual advisor to Nelson Mandela and the people of South Africa in the fight to end apartheid; To create peace in the Middle East;

- To reform the Church;

- To control the spread of HIV;

- Against poverty;

- Against war;

- To free Tibet; and

- To end human rights abuses in Zimbabwe.

First inspired by the mere tipping of a hat, Bishop Tutu had a significant impact on every one of these and many other issues. Nelson Mandela once summed up who Bishop Tutu is: "...sometimes strident, often tender, never afraid and seldom without humor...the voices of the voiceless."

ALTHOUGH SOUTH AFRICA HAS A LONG WAY TO GO TO SOLVE ITS ECONOMIC INEQUALITY, TODAY APARTHEID IS A THING OF THE PAST AND THE COUNTRY IS FREE AND DEMOCRATIC.

In the United States, a major reason for the success of the Civil Rights Movement in the 1960s was its Christian leadership. Three clerics – Reverend Martin Luther King, Jr., his chief strategist, Reverend Wyatt Walker, and his co-leader, the Reverend Fred Shuttlesworth, as members of the Southern Christian Leadership Conference – were among the visionary ministers who successfully promoted equality in civil rights. Christian clergy, nuns, student advocates, secular supporters and prominent members of the Jewish faith, and indeed of many faiths, followed their lead and supported them.

Septima Poinsette Clark, a committed Christian from Charleston, South Carolina, and the daughter of a slave, was among the most effective lay supporters of the movement. Through her efforts, the SCLC's set up 800 schools to teach citizenship to African Americans – so that they could pass the tests then necessary to vote in many states. She has been nicknamed the "mother" of the Civil Rights Movement.

Rev. Martin Luther King, Jr. (1929-1968) *Rev. Wyatt Walker (1929-)*

The SCLC's President, Reverend Martin Luther King, was a fourth generation minister, and Southern black churches served as the centers for the Civil Rights movement. As for the Christian genesis of the movement's moral code, Dr. King wrote in his "Letter From a Birmingham Jail" on April 16, 1963:

One may well ask, "How can you advocate breaking some laws and obeying others?" The answer is found in the fact that there are two types of laws: There are just laws and there are unjust laws. I would be the first to advocate obeying just laws. ... [But] I would agree with St. Augustine that "An unjust law is no law at all."

Rev. Fred Shuttlesworth (1922-2011)   *Septima Poinsette Clark (1898-1987)*

Ultimately, it took a level of courage more powerful than adults could muster to prevail in the Civil Rights Movement. It took the courage of children – namely some 3,500 high-schoolers who left school on May 2, 1963 to join in the Birmingham, Alabama demonstrations, when the adults were fearful of losing their jobs if they participated. When those children were bullied by Birmingham's Commissioner of Public Safety, Bull Connor, with his police dogs and high-pressure fire hoses, and the confrontation was broadcast on television worldwide, the protest movement had finally seized the moral high ground in the eyes of the American public.

The SCLC's and the Civil Rights movement's work in the 1960's led to the Civil Rights Act of 1964, the Voting Rights Act of 1965, and the Fair Housing Act of 1968, each of which substantially promoted equality in America.

When the Reverend King was given the Nobel Peace Prize in 1964, he insisted that Septima Poinsette Clark accompany him to Norway for the ceremony.

Today, Martin Luther King Jr. is a national hero, with a holiday named in his honor. What is often forgotten is that in his own lifetime, even as he succeeded, he was considered controversial – and not just in the deep South. A poll in 1966 found that 72% of white Americans viewed him unfavorably. It was faith that sustained him and allowed him to persevere despite a lack of popular support among much of the then white establishment in America.

Like Eleanor Roosevelt, Martin Luther King Jr. will be on the back of many five dollar bills in a few years.

ALTHOUGH ENORMOUS PROGRESS REMAINS TO BE ACCOMPLISHED, IN A POLL IN 2014, 80% OF AMERICANS AGREED THAT REAL PROGRESS IN ENDING RACIAL DISCRIMINATION WAS MADE AS A RESULT OF THE CIVIL RIGHTS MOVEMENT.

Other influential human and animal rights organizations, like Amnesty International, were also originally formed by Christians, or inspired by Christian principles. The primary founder of Amnesty International, for example, was Peter Benenson, a devout Christian.

Without Christianity, it is simply impossible to know the extent to which these seminal advances in human rights, civil rights and animal rights would still have occurred, when, or to what degree. Each one of these devout Christians and Christian groups led the way.

—— CHAPTER 9 ——

THANK YOU FOR FREEING AND RECREATING INDIA, THE WORLD'S SECOND MOST POPULOUS COUNTRY, IN THE 20TH CENTURY

(BLESSED ARE THOSE WHO ARE PERSECUTED BECAUSE OF RIGHTEOUSNESS)

Mahatma Gandhi (1869-1948)

Mahatma Gandhi described himself as a committed Hindu, although many have argued that he was a Christian in values and practice. Regardless, he earns a place in this book because he both utilized and taught the Christian world a thing or two about the meaning of Christ's teachings, of which he was undeniably a devoted student; and also because he analyzed, admired and followed the Beatitudes. Thus, notwithstanding recent revelations about his odd personal habits and opinions, and whether or not he was a literal Christian, he was certainly a "Beatitudinal Christian" in his public actions.

As a young man in South Africa, by 'coincidence,' Gandhi was taken to regular services at a Methodist church. He soon became enamored by Christ's teachings, which he thought most Christians failed to live up to. "It does not matter to me," he once said, "if someone demonstrated that the man Jesus never lived and that what we read in the Gospels is nothing more than a production of the author's imagination. The Sermon on the Mount will always remain true in my eyes." He further loved and expressly stated that he considered Jesus simply the most influential person ever to walk the Earth:

An example of this flowering may be found in the figure and in the life of Jesus. I refuse to believe that there now exists or has ever existed a person that has not made use of his example to lessen his sins, even though he may have done so without realizing it. The lives of all have, in some greater or lesser degree, been changed by his presence, his actions, and the words spoken by his divine voice.

- M. K. GANDHI, "WHAT JESUS MEANS TO GANDHIJI." THE MODERN REVIEW, OCTOBER 1941.

When it came time to confront the British colonial occupation of India, Gandhi chose to follow Christ's teachings on non-violence as his method of rebellion. As he explained:

And there are others who affirm; 'Christianity has become a pretense at present. Christians do not understand the message of Jesus. It is necessary to deliver it over again in the way we can under-

stand.'... But I must say that so long as we do not accept the principle of loving the enemy, all talk of world brotherhood is an airy nothing.

- Speech by M. K. Gandhi to London Missionary Society of India in 1925.

Ultimately, the British became powerless to fight Gandhi, so perfectly did he adopt the principles of their own religion and demonstrate it for them.

Gandhi never won the Nobel Peace Prize, due to political squabbles. He was scheduled to receive the Prize in 1948, but on January 30, 1948, he was killed for his nonviolent views, which the assassin is said to have believed were emasculating Hinduism. It was the sixth assassination attempt on his life, the others being in 1934, two in 1944, in 1946, and earlier in January of 1948. As an honor to him, upon his death, no Prize at all was awarded that year, on the grounds that there was no equally suitable candidate.

❦

Behind the scenes, one of Gandhi's closest religious advisors was the Reverend Eli Stanley Jones. Called the "Billy Graham of India," he was a Christian missionary who cared for the lowest castes in India. Christianity never took full root in India, in part because it could not overcome its deeply held caste system. Reverend Jones

Rev. Eli Stanley Jones (1884-1973)

persevered nonetheless, and achieved considerable success. Without degredating India's native religions, he simply preached that the Gospel of Jesus was meant for the entire world, even the lowest on the socioeconomic ladder.

Jones preached to Gandhi, and all who would listen, that the Beatitudes were his country's path to freedom in his book, <u>The Christ of the Mount: A Working Philosophy of Life</u> (1931) (the title referring to the Sermon on the Mount, which again contained the Beatitudes). And listen Gandhi did. As Jones remarked on Gandhi's life:

A little man in a loin cloth in India picks out from the Sermon on the Mount one of its central principles, applies it as a method for gaining human freedom, and the world, challenged and charmed, bends over to catch the significance of the great sight. It is a portent of what would happen if we would take the whole of the Sermon on the Mount and apply it to the whole of life. It would renew our Christianity—it would renew the world. Our present-day Christianity, anemic and weak from the parasites that have fastened themselves on its life through the centuries,

*needs a blood-transfusion from the Sermon on the
Mount in order to renew radiant health within it that
it may throw off these parasites and arise to serve
and save the world.*

Reverend Jones is also credited with influencing
Gandhi and other Indian leaders to ensure that post-inde-
pendence India permitted full religious freedom.

'Coincidentally,' it was Reverend Jones' biography
of Gandhi entitled <u>Gandhi: Portrayal of a Friend</u> (1948),
which inspired Martin Luther King to rely solely upon
nonviolence in the United States Civil Rights Movement.

Today, India is independent, religiously free under its
constitution and democratic.

—— CHAPTER 10 ——

THANK YOU FOR PRESERVING AN UNDER-GROUND MOVEMENT FOR RELIGIOUS FREEDOM IN CHINA, THE WORLD'S MOST POPULOUS COUNTRY, IN THE 20TH CENTURY

(BLESSED ARE THOSE WHO
ARE PERSECUTED BECAUSE OF
RIGHTEOUSNESS)

ommunist party docu-
ments in China marked
'top secret,' which have
now been released, reveal how
years of underground activity
by the Jesuits and other Catholic
priests preceded a crackdown in
1955. That year, Cardinal (then
Bishop) Ignatius Kung Pin-Mei
of Shanghai, along with 1,200
other leading Catholics, were
arrested and imprisoned.

Cardinal Ignatius Kung Pin-Mei
(1901-2000)

Months later, brought with
his hands tied behind his back to
address a crowd at a dog-racing
stadium, and told to direct his fellow Catholics to accede
to government control, he shocked his captors with a sud-
den outburst into the microphone:

Long live Christ the King and
Long live the Pope.

The stunned crowd soon turned it into a chant.

It was four years before Cardinal Kung was even
seen in public again. The purpose of his next public exposure was to put him on trial, and to sentence him to life
in prison. In 1979, the Vatican made then Bishop Kung a
Cardinal *in pectore*, Latin for "in secret," to protect him
from further punishment. His ascension to that position
was not made public until 1991, after he was out of China.

Cardinal Kung served in China, largely in solitary con-
finement, for 30 years, but never broke his allegiance to his

faith, and thereby inspired millions of Catholic followers.

Christianity came to China in the 7th century. Originally the religion of the peasants, today it is seeing its fastest growth along the East Coast and in cities among the more educated and prosperous. Starting in the 1980s more than one-hundred million migrant workers flocked from rural farming communities to China's burgeoning cities and brought their Christian beliefs with them. Christianity is still viewed by the majority of Chinese as a 'foreign religion,' so there is a high degree of tension and social and cultural discrimination between the non-Christian urban Chinese and the growing community of rural migrant workers. However, migrant workers have managed to start forming their own Christian churches in these growing cities. These churches have built a social network that allows the transitioning immigrants to more easily adapt to their new city lives and to express their emotions and frustrations in a safe environment. Urban churches are also now gaining members, not just from migrant workers, but also the more highly educated and social elites. Also, some of the main leaders of today's Chinese Catholic Church are women, with a strong Pentecostal influence.

In 1949, at the time the Communists took control, the country had 5,700 Catholic foreign missionaries. From 1966 to 1979, largely under Chairman Mao Zedong, China banned all religion in any form – the only country in the world besides Albania to do so. Even today, it is illegal for Chinese Christians and foreign Christians to hold formal meetings. In recent years, under leader Xi Jinping, the crackdown has been the fiercest in decades. *The New York Times* reported in 2016 that since 2014 Chinese authorities have removed 1,700 crosses from churches in Zhejiang province, a hotbed of Christianity, because of the concern that they had come to "dominate" the skyline. The fact that 1,700 public crosses had been placed outdoors in a single Chinese province, and that the government saw them as such a threat that they needed to be forcefully removed, reminiscent of Poland in the next chapter, tells you everything that you need to know about the rise in the popularity of Christianity in 21st century China.

That popularity became even stronger when Chinese Christians responded with great charity to the 7.9-magnitude 2008 Sichuan earthquake, which killed as many as 90,000 people. For example, even though the Protestant Church in Mianzhu was damaged beyond repair, the 180-member congregation nonetheless started a medical clinic and 'gospel choir,' and offered counseling. The Christian response caused the entire country to take notice – Christian churches in Sichuan saw dramatic increases in conversions. History is thus repeating itself. You will recall that it was the enormous charity of the early Christians in creating hospitals that converted the Roman Empire; the same boundless love is now converting Communist China. Given China's historic one child policy, the vast majority of Christian growth has had to come through conversions.

As one author has explained:

The growth of Christianity in China has been astonishing. At this point, it's no longer a question of if China will become a Christian nation, but when. The ramifications of this religious shift are massive, and will shake China's culture and economy to their cores.

Since 1979, Protestant Christianity has been growing in China at a compound annual growth rate of more than 10 percent. There were 3 million Christians in China in 1980, compared to 58 million in 2010, according to Fenggyang Yang, director of the Center of Religion and Chinese Society at Purdue University. By 2025, that number could swell to 250 to 300 million.

Surprised? That makes sense. The Chinese Communist Party has done all it can to downplay this phenomenon and keep a tight media lid on it. Meanwhile, Western media outlets are so taken with the idea that religion is an irrelevant (and declining) facet of modern life that they don't pay attention to its growth in most places outside calcified Western Europe.

But this shift is happening, and it is astonishing, especially considering that China is officially an atheist country.

- PASCAL-EMMANUEL GOBRY, "CAN CHRISTIANITY SAVE CHINA?" THE WEEK, JULY 14, 2016.

Sadly, even amidst Christianity's rapid growth, the same type of severe persecution that Cardinal Kung suffered is still going on today in China. Hu Shigen, age 61, of Tianjin, is a Christian who has led several underground churches. In August of 2016, he was sentenced to more than seven years in prison for spreading "subversive thoughts and ideas" using "illegal" religious groups, according to Xinhua, China's state-run news agency. He previously served a 16-year prison term for helping to publicize the truth about the Chinese government's assault upon student protesters near Tiananmen Square in 1989. A prominent Christian lawyer, Zhang Kai, 36, who had been challenging China's removal of crosses in Zhejiang province, was also arrested in 2015 just before a planned meeting with the U.S. ambassador-at-large for religious freedom, and in 2016 was put on television to confess publicly for his crimes, sparking outrage. These are just a few examples of this counter-trend.

On a more positive note, there was one surprising development that occurred on August 4th, 2015. On that date, Father Joseph Zhang Yinlin, an auxiliary bishop of Weihui, was consecrated with the joint approval of the Vatican and the Chinese government – progress in allowing the Vatican to participate in the appointment of bishops, a point of contention for the previous 60 years. Whether that development may lead to more leniency toward Christians by future governments remains to be seen.

Christmas in China today is also the country's most popular holiday – among all segments of the population.

CHINA TODAY HAS AN ESTIMATED 67 MILLION TO 100 MILLION CHRISTIANS—COMPARED TO ONLY 87 MILLION COMMUNIST PARTY MEMBERS. THE NUMBER IS GROWING SO FAST THAT, AS NOTED ABOVE, SOME HAVE ESTIMATED IT COULD REACH AS MANY AS 250 MILLION BY 2030, DESPITE THE CRACKDOWN, AND EVEN AS MORE OF THE DEVOUT GO UNDERGROUND, WHICH COULD WELL MAKE IT THE LARGEST CHRISTIAN COMMUNITY IN THE WORLD IN THE NEXT TWO DECADES.

—— CHAPTER 11 ——

THANK YOU FOR HELPING TO DEFEAT TOTALITARIANISM IN COMMUNIST EUROPE IN THE 20TH CENTURY

(BLESSED ARE THOSE WHO ARE PERSECUTED BECAUSE OF RIGHTEOUSNESS)

A mong the most influential figurative foot soldiers and generals, who have to be credited, along with others, with helping to defeat communist control of Eastern Europe in the 20th century, were Father Jerzy Popieluszko and Pope John Paul II.

Poland has been Christian since the year 966, when their King was baptized. The faith of the Polish people was solidified in 1655, when a 3,000-man strong army from Sweden was defeated by several hundred soldiers, civilians and monks. The victory was attributed to the intercession of Mary, Jesus' mother, said to be the Protectress of Poland. The icon of a 'Black Madonna' was thereafter housed in the Jasna Góra Monastery and it became the country's symbol of faith.

Father Jerzy Popieluszko was a mere 34 years old in 1981 when he was asked, due to the 'coincidental' absence of a more senior priest, to celebrate Mass at the Solidarity shipyard. These shipyard workers at the time were leading the challenge to Soviet Communist control of Poland. As Father Jerzy entered the shipyard, his main concern

Father Jerzy Popieluszko (1947-1984)

was how he would manage such a large mass. As he entered, the workers rose in thunderous applause. Who, he wondered, had arrived to cause them to cheer? As he put it, "At first I thought there was somebody important be-hind me..." He then looked over his shoulder. When he saw no celebrity, he soon realized, to his astonishment, that they were cheering for him. They were cheering be-cause, as a priest, he had the courage to come and min-ister to them despite strong Communist opposition to the Church. Where had his courage come from? His hero was Father Maximillian Kolbe, discussed earlier in this book.

From that day forward, Father Jerzy's powerful ser-mons, many broadcast on radio, demanding religious and political freedom, united the Polish people. In a sermon which would presage his own death, Father Jerzy said simply of Communism: "An idea which needs rifles to survive dies of its own accord."

Becoming more outspoken, even as the violence grew, Father Jerzy composed extraordinarily meaning-ful prayers of protest and protection to Mary, the mother of Jesus:

Mother of those who place their hope in Solidarity,
*   pray for us.*
Mother of those who are deceived, pray for us.
Mother of those who are betrayed, pray for us.
Mother of those who are arrested in the night, pray
*   for us.*
Mother of those who are imprisoned, pray for us.
Mother of those who suffer from the cold, pray
*   for us.*
Mother of those who have been frightened, pray

for us.
Mother of those who were subjected to
    interrogations, pray for us.
Mother of those innocents who have been
    condemned, pray for us.
Mother of those who speak the truth, pray for us.
Mother of those who cannot be corrupted, pray
    for us.
Mother of those who resist, pray for us.
Mother of orphans, pray for us.
Mother of those who have been molested because
    they wore your image, pray for us.
Mother of those who are forced to sign declarations
    contrary to conscience, pray for us.
Mother of mothers who weep, pray for us.
Mother of fathers who have been so deeply
    saddened, pray for us.
Mother of suffering Poland, pray for us.
Mother of always faithful Poland, pray for us.

In 1982, Poland's Communist leadership leaned on its Archbishop Jozef Glemp to try to silence Father Jerzy. Glemp, who called Father Jerzy's sermons a source of "useless friction with the State," complied, ordering him to study in Rome. However, due to Vatican bureaucracy – Father Jerzy was situated in another archdiocese not technically headed up by Archbishop Glemp – the move was delayed. Ultimately, Pope John Paul II himself rejected the transfer. Instead, he sent Father Jerzy his personal rosary beads, and words of encouragement.

When in May of 1983, the Polish Security Police brutally murdered a member of the Communist opposition – a student – it was Father Jerzy's voice that echoed the steely resolve of an entire nation:

This nation is not forced to its knees by any satanic power. This nation has proved that it bends the knee only to God. And for that reason we believe that God will stand up for it.

The Communist State's fears of Father Jerzy's's outspoken views ultimately led the Polish secret police to attack him. First, they spread insinuations of scandal into newspaper stories. Anti-government literature was later planted in his apartment, and he was arrested and held for two days. His living quarters were bombed. Finally, in 1984, he was kidnapped. The entire nation held its breath for ten days and a round-the-clock vigil was held in his Church. Ultimately, his body was found in the Vistula reservoir; he had been beaten to death. His beating had been so brutal that he had choked on his own blood and vomit, while gagged.

The Secret Police no doubt expected that now that the pesky priest was gone, he would be forgotten. After all, he was just a young parish priest. And, like Jesus, his entire public ministry had been only about three years long.

However, something happened that the Communist authorities had not counted on. In death, Father Jerzy's message rang even louder. Six bishops came to celebrate this low level priest's funeral. And 1,000 priests. And over 250,000 people. (To imagine the size of that crowd, picture the throngs who filled the Washington Mall for Martin Luther King's "I Have a Dream" speech – and then add 50,000).

Something else also happened. In Father Jerzy's name, those people now demanded freedom. As one scholarly work has since explained, after his death, the Polish State simply lost control:

[B]ooklets of Popieluszko's sermons arrived from underground printers, titled in the distinctive lettering of the Solidarity logo, and were handed out in churches. Soviet leader [Konstantin] Chernenko wrote to [Polish leader Wojciech] Jaruzelski, "All the hostile elements are receiving support and protection from the Church.... The Church is now directly defying the socialist state.... It is preparing a counterrevolutionary army in the full sense of the word."

Chernenko was absolutely right. But with the Soviet economy in tatters, his own army bogged down in Afghanistan, and his population disgusted, there was nothing he could do about it.

-JONATHAN KWITNY, MAN OF THE CENTURY: THE LIFE AND TIMES OF POPE JOHN PAUL II (1997).

Pope John Paul II personally visited Father Jerzy's grave in June, 1987. Five years after his death, in 1989, the Communist party finally relented and relinquished control of Poland – and later even the Soviet Union.

Pope John Paul II (1920-2005)

Father Jerzy's commitment to free Poland is not forgotten; his beatification mass in 2010 drew another 150,000 people.

⁂

In 1979, just eight months into his papacy, Pope John Paul II rallied Poland in a profound way, drawing crowds for one mass of 500,000 people, part of 13 million Poles who saw him live (37% of the entire populace) during that single trip. His words of encouragement: "Do not be afraid," to a crowd which chanted back "We want God," made him the spiritual leader of the entire Soviet bloc.

As for Pope John Paul's influence on the fall of Communism, the agnostic British historian, Timothy Garton Ash, has opined:

No one can prove conclusively that he was a primary cause of the end of communism...I would argue the historical case in three steps: without the Polish Pope, no Solidarity revolution in Poland in 1980; without Solidarity, no dramatic change in Soviet

policy towards eastern Europe under Gorbachev;
without that change, no velvet revolutions in 1989.

- Timothy Garton Ash. "The Greatest Political Actor of Our Time Leaves Us The Challenge of Moral
Globalization." The Guardian, April 4, 2005.

Paul Johnson, in his book *Heroes: From Alexander the
Great and Julius Caesar to Churchill and De Gaulle,* explains why John Paul succeeded, without firing a shot, in
playing a central role in defeating the Soviet juggernaut:

Once his ghostly leadership on the actual soil of
Poland was firmly established, there was never any
possibility of Soviet imperial rule reestablishing
itself without a bloodbath of a kind not even Bresh-
nev would have been prepared to face, and all his
successors flunked totally. In many ways, it was the
most impressive display of papal political power
since the time of Innocent III in the early thirteenth
century, and gave the true answer to Stalin's brutal
(and foolish) question: "How many divisions has
the pope?"

On May 13, 1981, a recently released Turkish prisoner, and professional assassin, Mehmet Ali Ağca, also
a former member of the Turkish terrorist group the Gray

Wolves, shot four bullets and struck the Pope twice at close range with a Browning Hi-Power semi-automatic pistol. Four bullets; close range; professional assassin. One bullet just missed his aorta by inches. Miraculously, John Paul survived. The Pope, ardently devoted to Mary, the mother of Jesus, since the death of his own mother at age 9, attributed his survival to her intervention.

'Coincidentally,' May 13th is also the date when, in 1917, Mary is said to have first appeared to three young shepherd children in Fátima, Portugal. John Paul thereafter made several trips there to thank Mary for her intervention in saving his life. In 1983, he met with and forgave his would-be assassin.

An Italian investigatory commission concluded in 2006 that the Soviet KGB, fearful of the Pope's influence, was actually behind the assassination attempt.

> AS OF 1991, ALL SEVEN OF THE STATES IN THE COMMUNIST EASTERN BLOC (INCLUDING POLAND), AND ALL 15 OF THE FORMER SOVIET REGIONS, HAD LIBERATED THEMSELVES FROM THE CONTROL OF THE SOVIET UNION, WHICH ALSO DISSOLVED ITSELF.

—— CHAPTER 12 ——

THANK YOU FOR PROMOTING, THROUGH FREE ENTERPRISE, THE MORAL ECONOMY, IN THE 12TH THROUGH 20TH CENTURIES

(BLESSED ARE THOSE WHO HUNGER AND THIRST FOR RIGHTEOUSNESS)

L ike hospitals and schools, many historians now accept that the Christian monasteries of Europe were also partially responsible for at least the incubation of capitalism.

The High Middle Ages (1100-1300) was a period of great technological innovation – from clocks to new modes of transportation. The issue was how to get these then startling inventions into the hands of the masses, given that nearly a third of all of the land in Europe was owned by the Catholic Church. At the same time, large new sub-communities within the Church were sprouting up – including the Franciscan and Dominican orders. To protect their rights, Canon law in turn developed the legal

Pope Leo XIII (1810-1903)

principle of independent communities – the precursor to the first modern corporations.

Thus, in conjunction with and even before the sprouting of modern Protestant cities, the locations where Max Weber in <u>The Protestant Ethic and the Spirit of Capitalism</u> (1905) placed its origins, the foundation of institutionally organized free enterprise was already thriving in monasteries. Believing in the nobility of labor, the armies of monks in existence at the time cleared vast tracts of land for agriculture. In these same monestaries, the first factories and mills, hydraulically powered, grinding corn and producing wool, among other items of sale, began to manufacture and transport such items to market in large quantities. With their vibrant spirit, they further built roads and bridges to move their products, and promoted fairs to sell them. Thus, the first well-organized example of capitalism began.

Centuries later, Pope Leo XIII's 1891 encyclical, *Rerum novarum*, served as the intellectual and theological foundation for the reform of free enterprise, which Pope Francis refers to today as the "moral economy," and for social activism among Christians. It came as the bookend to his parallel prior encyclical, *Quod Apostolici Muneris* (1878), where the Church outright rejected socialism. It accepted capitalism, but demanded balance in its application.

The encyclical could not have been timelier, arriving in a time of dramatic social upheaval, questioning and uncertainty, sandwiched around Karl Marx and Frederick Engels' <u>Communist Manifesto</u> in 1848, Marx's <u>Das</u>

Kapital, finished in 1883, Germany's Social Democratic Party's calls for an 8 hour workday in 1891, the economic boom of the Second Industrial Revolution (bringing both railroads and skyscrapers), and the first Russian Revolution in 1905.

In its preamble, Pope Leo laid out his cards early, and pulled no punches:

> *[A] small number of very rich men have been able to lay upon the teeming masses of the labouring poor a yoke which is very little better than slavery itself ... The conflict now raging derives from the vast expansion of industrial pursuits and the marvellous discoveries of science; from the changed relations between masters and workmen; from the enormous fortunes of some few individuals and the utter poverty of the masses; from the increased self-reliance and closer mutual combination of working classes; and also, finally, from the prevailing moral degeneracy.*

Pope John XXIII called *"Rerum novarum"* the *Magna Carta* of Catholic doctrine, and it is customary to date the start of Catholic social teaching with its publication. *Rerum novarum* powerfully set forth not just what the Church rejected in economic structures, but also what it required:

> **Rerum Novarum** *was a mixture of a stress on the rights of property, reflections on the role of the state*

*in social affairs, an argument in favour of the need
to improve the wretched state of the works in the
industrial revolution, a defence of free association
among workers and others, a justification of the
right of the Church to intervene in political and
social affairs, and a concern to draw attention to the
exigencies of the 'common good.' The teaching put
forward was asserted to come from revelation and
natural law.*

-PAUL FURLONG AND DAVID CURTIS, THE CHURCH
FACES THE MODERN WORLD: RERUM NOVARUM AND ITS
IMPACT (1994).

Rerum novarum's teachings provided a moral and
theological basis for generations of subsequent worldwide social justice reform and propelled the growth of
unions. In the United States, after that encyclical, and for
various other reasons, Catholics joined unions in droves,
and union membership surged from less than 5% of the
non-self employed workforce in the 1890s to over 30%
by 1950.

The encyclical (like John Locke's writings) rein-
forced the Christian basis for property rights, grounded
in the theology that all people are created in the image
of God. The encyclical awakened middle class Catholics to the challenges of worker rights, urbanization and
industrialization – urging them to avoid the extremes of
both socialism and laissez faire capitalism. This inspired
a movement known as distributism, advocating private
property ownership, but admonishing that it should be

widely distributed.

Rerum novarum was followed closely by Walter Rauschenbusch's classic book, <u>Christianity and the Social Crisis</u> (1907), which served as another compelling statement of faith-based progressivism and offered a comprehensive argument for the social application of the Gospels. Together, these intellectual developments demonstrated that Christian teachings could be put to use to prevent suffering, a sentiment that laid the philosophical foundation (combined with other influences) for much of the socially conscious legislation in the United States that followed in that century.

In 2013, in his first year as Pope, Pope Francis echoed the works of Pope Leo when he issued his apostolic exhortation *"Evangelii Gaudium,"* (the "joy of the Gospel") in which he decried the "idolatry of money," and ridiculed "trickle-down economics" as "crude and naïve." Francis instead called for action to address historic levels of income inequality, with some describing his views as a powerful new gospel delineating the 'structural sins' of capitalism.

The Church thus, despite having over the centuries a complex relationship with capitalism, the details of which go beyond the scope of this book—for centuries it opposed charging interest—ultimately successfully helped to preserve economic freedom, as an alternative to avoid the extreme state control implicit in full-fledged socialism and communism. All along, it has still insisted (with varying degrees of success) upon a more humane distribution of wealth.

*Mary Harris "Mother" Jones
(1837-1930)*

If it was Pope Leo who laid out the theories of economic justice, it was Mary Harris Jones (known as "Mother Jones") who did the leg work to create it. She may have begun her career as a simple Irish-American dressmaker, but this devout Christian rose to become a world renowned labor and community organizer. She co-founded the Industrial Workers of the World in 1905, whose immodest goal was to include all the workers of the world in one single union.

Her public life began after her dress shop was burned down by the Great Chicago Fire of 1871, which she herself narrowly escaped. Her own life had never been easy, as prior to that, she had lost her husband and four children to yellow fever. A strong influence on her activism was her brother, Father William Richard Harris, a Catholic pastor.

She perservered as a labor leader. In 1903, she led a 'Children's Crusade' for the first child labor restrictions, by leading a 125-mile march of child workers from Pennsylvania to Teddy Roosevelt's vacation home in New York. At the time, an estimated one-sixth of American children under age 16 had been forced into full-time employment to survive. Mother Jones' demand was simple, and today seems unfathomable to oppose: the simple option for young children to choose to go to school rather than work. Many of the children who walked by her side that day had lost fingers or had other uncompensated work disabilities. Ultimately, sixty children completed the long trek and triumphantly walked up Second Avenue by torchlight.

The march had the desired effect. In 1904, a National Child Labor Committee was formed. A year later, Pennsylvania toughened its child labor laws. Ultimately, the New Deal presidency of Franklin D. Roosevelt passed nationwide legislation protecting young workers, the Fair Labor Standards Act of 1938.

Mother Jones was to minors in the early 1900s what Cesar Chavez was to become to migrant farm workers decades later. But she never took herself too seriously. Once, when introduced at a rally as a "great humanitarian," she promptly corrected the speaker, advising that he really didn't understand who she was: "I'm a hellraiser."

Cesar Chavez (1927-1993)

It was one Father Donald McDonnell who first read Leo XIII's encyclical *Rerum novarum* to Cesar Chavez. Father McDonnell also introduced Chavez to Gandhi and Dorothy Day. Soon, Chavez was helping him with mass in California farm workers' camps.

For three decades, starting in 1952, Cesar Chavez was at the forefront of the fight of migrant farm workers in America for a just living wage. Utilizing both Catholic doctrine and non-violent protest, including pilgrimages, fasting (such as a 25-day hunger strike) and Marian devotion (commitment to Jesus' mother Mary), he created the first migrant farm workers' union, and led strikes by the National Farm Worker's Association (NFWA). Ultimately, migrant farmers established a minimum wage above $1.20 per hour, and were granted for the first time the right to rest periods, clean water and protection from pesticide exposure.

Chavez used the power of non-violent protest – boycotts, strikes and hunger strikes – to effect change. When he drafted the Constitution of the United Farm Workers of America (successor to the NFWA), he took language straight from the Catholic Church's social teachings.

Every major initiative launched by Chavez began with a prayer, and images of Our Lady of Guadalupe preceded every march. When he died in 1993, a local farmer said simply, "The angels came and took him."

TODAY, MINIMUM WAGE LAWS EXIST IN ALL 50 STATES.

Thus, over the centuries, capitalism was launched, and ultimately dramatically reshaped, in part at least, by Christians and Christian principles.

——— CHAPTER 13 ———

THANK YOU FOR LAYING THE GROUNDWORK TO KEEP OUR PLANET SAFE FROM ENVIRONMENTAL HARM IN THE 21ST CENTURY

(BLESSED ARE THE PURE IN HEART)

Dorothy Stang (1931-2005)

S ister Dorothy Stang and Pope Francis are among the foot soldiers and generals in the 21st century who have begun to rally the world to fight environmental damage and climate change.

Sister Stang, a member of the Sisters of Notre Dame, taught school in Chicago and Phoenix before moving to Brazil. Seeing the vast poverty and lack of educational opportunity, she partnered with the Project for Sustainable Development, a government program, to encourage landless families to do sustainable farming, building what today have become 85 Christian communities containing 115 new one-room schools.

She soon took up residence in the Amazon Rain Forest, an area the size of the Continental United States. It has been referred to as the "Earth's lungs" because it fosters a critical exchange of gases necessary to the health of the planet, and it was being spoliated. Sister Dorothy saw how loggers, land speculators and cattle ranchers were damaging vast portions of the Rain Forest, threatening the world environment, while the Brazilian government stood by silently. Sister stood up to the predators, and that soon earned her a place on their feared "death list." Hired killings of environmentalists had already become all too common. Yet she persevered.

Despite receiving death threats for speaking out, she refused to be silent. Finally, Sister Dorothy was accosted in 2005 in the Rain Forest by two men who addressed her merely as "Sister" and asked if she had any weapons. She replied "yes" and indicated that her weapons were the Beatitudes. As she recited them, she was shot no less than six times and killed.

TODAY, THE PACE OF DESTRUCTION OF THE AMAZON RAIN FOREST IS AT ITS LOWEST RATE IN MORE THAN TWO DECADES. ITS PRESERVATION HAS BEEN REFERRED TO AS ONE OF THE GREATEST ENVIRONMENTAL PROGRESS STORIES ON THE PLANET.

In June 2015, Pope Francis issued an encyclical on climate change, called "*Laudato Si*" or "Praise Be to You," which called for a unified worldwide campaign to combat this peril. "If we destroy Creation," Francis said, "Creation will destroy us." And he added:

It must be said that some committed and prayerful Christians, with the excuse of realism and pragma-

tism, tend to ridicule expressions of concern for the environment. Others are passive; they choose not to change their habits and thus become inconsistent. So what they all need is an "ecological conversion," whereby the effects of their encounter with Jesus Christ become evident in their relationship with the world around them. Living our vocation to be protectors of God's handiwork is essential to a life of virtue; it is not an optional or a secondary aspect of our Christian experience.

Pope Francis had timed his words with purpose. He knew that world leaders would be meeting in Paris in December of 2015 to address the climate change issue.

Sometimes, words matter. This was one of those times. In November of 2015, the Yale Program on Climate Change Communication issued the results of its study called: *The Francis Effect: How Pope Francis Changed the Conversation About Global Warming.* It found that many Americans (17%) and Catholics (35%) were influenced by *Laudato Si* in their views on global warming. The Yale Study further concluded:

Of those Americans who say they've been influenced, half (50%) say the Pope's position on global warming made them more concerned about global warming...

As it turned out, the rest of the world, including world

Pope Francis (1936–)

leaders, were influenced in similar ways. Six months after the encyclical, the 195 world leaders who attended the December 2015 Paris conference on climate change passed, by consensus, the "Paris Agreement" to combat it.

In the last several decades, countless Catholic sisters (and priests), among many others across the world, have, like Pope Francis, dedicated themselves to care for the environment—playing an enormously successful role in changing attitudes worldwide.

AS NOTED, IN DECEMBER OF 2015, IN THE WAKE OF POPE FRANCIS' ENCYCLICAL "LAUDATO SI," WORLD LEADERS AGREED BY CONSENSUS TO THE LANDMARK GLOBAL "PARIS AGREEMENT" ON THE REDUCTION OF CLIMATE CHANGE, FOR THE FIRST TIME SETTING THE GOAL OF LIMITING GLOBAL WARMING TO LESS THAN 2 DEGREES CELSIUS. FURTHER VOTES ARE STILL REQUIRED IN THE INDIVIDUAL COUNTRIES TO IMPLEMENT IT.

—— CHAPTER 14 ——

THANK YOU FOR GIVING US THE GIFT OF THE GENTLE, GRACE-FILLED, SELFLESS AND SATISFYING INNER LIFE, STILL VIABLE IN THE 21ST CENTURY

(BLESSED ARE THE PURE IN HEART)

As we complete our historical review and 'thank you note' to Beatitudinal Christianity through the centuries, the pregnant question now, then, is do average people today still live – or even begin to live up to – the transformative work of these revolutionaries?

The answer is that yes, in ways large and small, we do. Here are some specific data, in the United States:

Forty percent of all regular churchgoers say they volunteered in the past year to help the poor or elderly, while only 15 percent of people who do not go to church say the same. Thirty-six percent of regular churchgoers volunteer with school or youth programs as compared to 15 percent of nonchurchgoers. Twenty-six percent of regular churchgoers have volunteered with a civic or neighborhood group, as opposed to 13 percent of nonchurchgoers. Twenty-one percent of regular churchgoers have worked on healthcare or some particular disease—that means they volunteer for a blood drive, or to help AIDS victims, or the American Heart Association campaign, or whatever—as compared to 13 percent of nonchurchgoers.

---

* * * *

Data from the General Social Survey show that (again controlling for other factors) religious people are more likely to give blood, to return excess change to a clerk, to give money to panhandlers, to spend time with someone who is "a bit down," and even to let a stranger cut in front of them in line. In short, it is not just in formal settings, but also in "informal altruism" that religious people are significantly more likely to step forward.

-ROBERT PUTNAM. "AMERICAN GRACE." THE TANNER LECTURES ON HUMAN VALUES. PRINCETON UNIVERSITY. 27-28 OCTOBER 2010.

> A 2013 GALLUP POLL FOUND THAT AMERICAN CHRISTIANS WERE 25% MORE LIKELY TO VOLUNTEER TIME TO A CHARITABLE CAUSE THAN PERSONS WITH NO RELIGIOUS AFFILIATIONS.

Persons strongly affiliated with religiously-based social networks show even higher community volunteerism. As explained by Robert Putnam and David Campbell in <u>American Grace: How Religion Divides and Unifies Us</u> (2010), that group is far more likely to join community groups, attend public meetings, work to solve community problems, to volunteer and to donate money (even to non-religious causes). The differences are significant:

- 43% of those with more religious social connections also belonged to three or more community groups, as compared to 15% of the less religiously connected people.

- 60% of those with more religious social connections attend public meetings, as compared to 37% of the less religiously connected people.

- 42% of those with more religious social connections had worked to solve a community problem, as compared to 20% of the less religiously connected people.

- 62% of those with more religious social connections had volunteered even for a non-religious group, as opposed to 35% of the less religiously connected people.

- 73% of those with more religious social connections had given money even for a non-religious cause, as opposed to 62% of the less religiously connected people.

A Pew Research Center Study issued in 2016 found that:

Highly religious people are distinctive in their day-to-day behaviors in several key ways: They are more engaged with their families, more involved in their communities and more likely to report being happy with the way things are going in their lives.

– PEW RESEARCH CENTER, APRIL 12, 2016, "RELIGION IN EVERYDAY LIFE."

The Pew Study further found that highly religious people were more likely to report being "very satisfied" with their life than atheists/agnostics (74% to 64%), significantly more likely to report being "very happy" (40% to 26%), and also significantly more likely to perform volunteer work (45% to 28%).

In their book <u>God is Back</u> (2009), John Micklethwait and Adrian Wooldridge opine that there is "considerable evidence that, regardless of wealth, Christians are healthier and happier than their secular brethren." Micklethwait and Wooldridge summarize: "One of the most striking results of the Pew Forum [Research Center]'s regular survey of happiness is that Americans who attend religious services once or more a week are happier (43 percent very happy) than those who attend monthly or less (31 percent) or seldom or never (26 percent). . . . The correlation between happiness and church attendance has been fairly steady since Pew started the survey in the 1970s; it is also more robust than the link between happiness and wealth."

Meanwhile, Peter Watson in <u>The Age of Atheists</u> (2014), laid out his own comprehensive summary of the statistical data:

Studies also show, they say, that religion can combat bad behavior as well as promote well-being. "Twenty years ago, Richard Freeman, a Harvard economist, found that black youths who attended church were more likely to attend school and less likely to commit crimes or use drugs." Since then, a host of further studies, including the 1991 report by the National Commission on Children, have concluded that religious participation is associated with lower rates of crime and drug use. James Q. Wilson (1931-2012), perhaps America's pre-eminent criminologist, succinctly summarized "a mountain of [social-scientific] evidence": "Religion, independent of social class, reduces deviance." Finally, Jonathan Gruber, "a secular-minded economist" at the Massachusetts Institute of Technology, has argued "on the basis of a mass of evidence" that churchgoing produces a boost in income.

While there is some contrary research, the balance of the carefully developed data – including the studies referenced by Stark, Putnam, Gallup, Pew and Watson – clearly support the value of a commitment to religion in general, and Christianity in particular. Thus, it would appear that, on the margin at least, enough Christians are living out the Beatitudes to make a difference in society.

If so, then another question is, what explains (other than some believe a boost from Divine Providence) why these teachings are still being followed two millennia after Christ's death? Could it be that, in the rare instance where it is attained, the psychological benefits of living life to the fullest meaning of Christian principles result in profound personal benefits? Or put another way, could the existence of a large cadre of people dedicated to true Christian living be both profoundly psychologically healthy and beneficial to society? We consider this issue in the next, and final, chapter.

—— CHAPTER 15 ——

THANK YOU FOR A PHILOSOPHY THAT INSPIRES THE HIGHEST LEVELS OF SPIRITUAL SELF-TRANSCENDENCE, MARKED BY UNCONDITIONAL FORGIVENESS, STILL VIABLE IN THE 21ST CENTURY

(BLESSED ARE THE PURE IN HEART)

"My strength is as the strength of ten, because my heart is pure."

- ALFRED TENNYSON, SIR GALAHAD

We return here again to the source of Beatitudinal Christianity – the Sermon on the Mount. Some theologians believe that the Beatitudes are listed in ascending order of sanctity. Like the rungs of a ladder, you must climb each one to lead you to the next. Let's repeat them again to consider that thesis:

> *Blessed are the poor in spirit, for theirs is the kingdom of Heaven.*
>
> *Blessed are those who mourn, for they will be comforted.*
>
> *Blessed are the meek, for they will inherit the earth.*
>
> *Blessed are those who hunger and thirst for righteousness, for they will be filled.*
>
> *Blessed are the merciful, for they will be shown mercy.*
>
> *Blessed are the pure in heart, for they will see God.*
>
> *Blessed are the peacemakers, for they will be called children of God.*
>
> *Blessed are those who are persecuted for righteousness' sake, for theirs is the kingdom of heaven.*

- MATTHEW 5:3-12

This progression makes sense as a hierarchy. We know instinctively that being poor in spirit – not constantly chasing material wealth – is a pre-condition to sanctity. By definition, if we fill our time attempting to pursue material gain, there is little time left for charitable pursuits. We know that enduring persecution requires a higher level of courage, for example, than merely being poor in spirit. Of course, any "sanctity hierarchy," must rank courageous actions highly, as C.S. Lewis explained in The Screwtape Letters (1942):

Courage is not simply one of the virtues, but the form of every virtue at the testing point, which means the point of highest reality.

In other words, under this theological hierarchy, the first step toward living a Christian life is to be "poor in spirit," followed by mourning for the suffering in the world. Once that suffering is internalized, we transform our outward life to live in brotherhood and sisterhood with the suffering, to strip ourselves of vanity; i.e., to live a 'meek' life. Then, once we are "poor in spirit," in "mourning," "meek," and we "hunger and thirst" for what is right – all of which are internal purification steps; then, and only then, do we break through the shell of inertia and move to the next logical steps: sacrificial, *ameliorative* external action.

Note Jesus' use of the phrase "hunger and thirst" for righteousness. This is more than just wishing it to be, or lamenting its absence. The true Christian has as urgent a desire for right in the world as a thirsty person in the desert has a desire for water.

Climbing the four rungs of the Beatitude's external actions is then, in order, to first show mercy, second to purify our hearts of excessive worldly needs, and, ultimately, to become active 'peacemakers,' until *paradoxically* we ourselves may even be 'persecuted'.

Showing 'mercy,' is not a passive act for a Christian. Indeed, over the centuries, the Catholic faith has identified seven "Corporal Works of Mercy," many of them taken from Jesus' parable of the Sheep and the Goats (Matthew 25:35-40), later codified by Thomas Aquinas, that we are called upon to live out in order to show true mercy:

THE SEVEN CORPORAL WORKS OF MERCY

- Feed the hungry
- Give drink to the thirsty
- Clothe the naked
- Shelter the homeless
- Comfort the imprisoned
- Visit the sick
- Bury the dead

A more contemporary Christian message by the Christian theologian Howard Thurman has its own list:

When the song of the angels is stilled,
When the star in the sky is gone,
When the kings and princes are home,
When the shepherds are back with their flocks,

The work of Christmas begins:
To find the lost,
To heal the broken,
To feed the hungry,
To release the prisoner,
To rebuild the nations,
To bring peace among brothers,
To make music in the heart.

- HOWARD THURMAN, "WHEN THE SONG OF THE ANGELS IS STILLED," THE MOOD OF CHRISTMAS AND OTHER CELEBRATIONS (1985).

The final stage in this upward progression up the 'rungs' of the Beatitudes then, in any given time, and given human nature, is to be so unrelenting in one's demands for righteous conduct as to sometimes become at some level 'persecuted because of righteousness.' What is ultimately asked of us, in this highest stage of commitment to true Christian principles, is to endure such persecution, and despite it, to remain a peacemaker.

The Beatitudes can thus be viewed as more than a prescription as to how to get to heaven; they can also be viewed when practiced *en masse* as step-by-step sequential directions – a MapQuest so to speak – setting out the pathway to achieve a better world.

These Beatitudes were not delivered in a vacuum, of course. They obviously came sequentially, biblically, after the Ten Commandments, a series of rules of 'right conduct.' Jesus did not reject the Ten Commandments. Nor do the Beatitudes; in fact, they reinforce one another. Rather, while the Ten Commandments delineate the proper bounds of external conduct, the Beatitudes supplement them by marking levels in the grace-filled development of the soul, and its external manifestations.

Thus, while the Ten Commandments are prohibitions designed to discipline us, so as to avoid doing interpersonal harm, the Beatitudes, in contrast, proscribe affirmative conduct, designed to bring us interpersonal (and societal) fulfillment. Clearly, then, for the Christian, compliance with the Ten Commandments alone is insufficient to create a full life, as Jesus himself makes manifest in the Gospel of Mark:

As Jesus was setting out on a journey again, a man ran up to him, knelt before him, and asked, "Good master, what must I do to have eternal life?" Jesus answered, "Why do you call me good? Nobody's good but God alone. But you know the commandments: Do not kill; do not commit adultery; do not steal; do not bear false witness; do not cheat; honor your mother and father," and the man replied, "I have obeyed all these commandments since my childhood."

Then Jesus looked steadily at him, and loved him, and he said, "For you, one thing is lacking: Go, sell what you have, give the money to the poor, then come and follow me." On hearing these words, [the man's] face fell and he went away sorrowful, for he was a man of great wealth.

- MARK 10:17-22

And the Beatitudes do not exist in a religious vacuum either. Scholars have written that the Eight Beatitudes have some (loose) parallels with the predecessor eightfold path of Buddhism to enlightenment. Consider:

EIGHTFOLD PATH	BEATITUDES
Right Understanding	*Blessed are the Poor in Spirit*
Right Thought	*Blessed are those who Mourn*
Right Speech	*Blessed are the Meek*
Right Action	*Blessed are those who hunger and thirst after Righteousness*
Right Livelihood	*Blessed are the Merciful*
Right Effort	*Blessed are the Pure in Heart*
Right Mindfulness	*Blessed are the Peacemakers*
Right Concentration	*Blessed are the Persecuted*

Thomas Merton, of course, famously linked mystically Christianity and Zen Buddhism in his work, <u>Zen</u>

and the Birds of Appetite (1968). Merton stated that he felt more in common with contemplative Buddhists than with non-contemplative Christians.

Similarly, Gandhi has written that the Beatitudes also reflect the best of Hinduism, declaring:

I have not been able to see any difference between the Sermon on the Mount and the Bkagavadgita [Bhagavad Gita]. What the Sermon describes in a graphic manner, the Bkagavadgita [Bhagavad Gita] reduces to a scientific formula. It may not be a scientific book in the accepted sense of the term, but it has argued out the law of love — the law of abandon as I would call it — in a scientific manner. The Sermon on the Mount gives the same law in wonderful language. The New Testament gave me comfort and boundless joy, as it came after the repulsion that parts of the Old had given me. Today supposing I was deprived of the Gita and forgot all its contents but had a copy of the Sermon, I should derive the same joy from it as I do from the Gita.

- M. K. GANDHI. "CEYLON MEMORIES: THINGS OF THE SPIRIT." YOUNG INDIA, VOL. IX, NO. 50 (DECEMBER 22, 1927).

The next critical question then is: does living one's life according to the Beatitudes, and thus arguably also in harmony with some of the best principles of Buddhist and

Hindu enlightenment, psychologically lead to more individual and societal fulfillment? To analyze that question, consider the parallels between the renowned psychologist Abraham Maslow's "Hierarchy of Needs," as the path to achieve personal fulfillment, and the Beatitudes. A life-long atheist, Maslow's hierarchy of needs, first proposed in his 1943 paper "A Theory of Human Motivation," has been described as "one of the most enduring contributions of psychology." That hierarchy is as follows:

——— SELF-TRANSCENDENCE ———

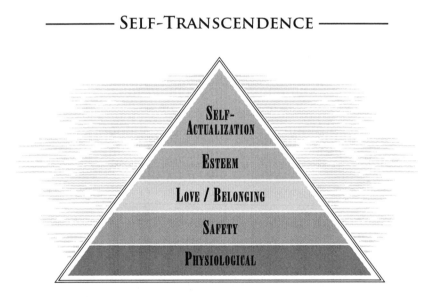

These six stages in Maslow's "Hierarchy of Needs," the pyramid of needs that every human must "climb" as he or she evolves to a higher level of consciousness (and conduct), are detailed as follows:

———— HIERARCHY OF NEEDS ————

1	PHYSIOLOGICAL (SURVIVAL) NEEDS	*Seeks to obtain the basic necessities of life*
2	SAFETY NEEDS	*Seeks security through order and law*
3	BELONGINGNESS AND LOVE NEEDS	*Seeks affiliation with a group*
4	ESTEEM NEEDS	*Seeks esteem through recognition or achievement*
5	SELF-ACTUALIZATION	*Seeks fulfillment of personal potential*
6	SELF-TRANSCENDENCE[8]	*Seeks to further a cause beyond the self and to experience a communion beyond the boundaries of the self through peak experience.*

According to the scholar Mark Koltko-Rivera, the highest level of self-awareness for Maslow was "self-transcendence, to further a cause beyond the self," a level that moves beyond mere egoistic self-actualization and

---

[8]   While early versions of Maslow's work identified only the bottom five levels, Mark E. Koltko-Rivera articulates how the sixth level was revealed in "Rediscovering the Later Version of Maslow's Hierarchy of Needs: Self-Transcendence and Opportunities for Theory, Research, and Unification." (2006).

esteem needs. Closely aligned, the highest level in living out the Beatitudes is the self-transcendent act of becoming a peacemaker – even if that requires bearing the burden of persecution. Put more simply, Maslow seems to have grasped (even without remotely accepting his divinity) the deep satisfaction and unparalleled joy that can be inherent in accepting Jesus' teachings. Maslow understood that, paradoxically, emotional health thrives as a result of sacrifice. He also surely, conversely, must have understood, as Thomas Merton stated, in <u>The Seven Storey Mountain</u> (1948), that for selfish souls: "The one who does most to avoid suffering [finds]…his very existence and consciousness…is his greatest torture."

For Koltko-Rivera, this then is where Maslow's self-transcendent level of being, and the living out of the Beatitudes to their highest level – becoming a peacemaker – finally intersect in the work of what he terms a "significant minority":

History has demonstrated that a significant minority of the human species functions primarily from the position that it is more important to serve some selfless greater purpose than to serve one's own purposes. (One thinks in this respect of the Mother Teresa's, Albert Schweitzer's, and Gandhi's of the world, as well as many lesser known individuals who put their lives at risk for social justice and environmental and religious causes.) A comprehensive theory of human personality and social behav-

ior must account for such individuals. There are, of course, various scientific approaches to altruism. The self-transcendence aspect of Maslow's theory should be seriously considered in relation to these issues. [Citations omitted].

Thus, Koltko-Rivera goes on to conclude, Maslow's "self-transcendence" and Christian "self-sacrifice" are actually two sides of the same coin:

On a somewhat different plane, the [Christian] sociologist Rodney Stark has asserted, on the basis of the historical record, that despite the association of monotheistic religion and violence, monotheistic religion has been a driving force behind social progress and the advance of science. It seems plausible that some of this effect might be associated with a motivational stance centered in [Maslow's] self-transcendence, putting aside self in favor of the greater good, the search for truth and so forth. [Citations omitted].

- Mark Koltko-Rivera, "Rediscovering the Later Version of Maslow's Hierarchy of Needs: Self-Transcendence and Opportunities for Theory, Research, and Unification." Review of General Psychology 10.4 (2006).

The next question is whether this attempt to equate living up to the highest level of Christianity's Beatitudes to living at the highest level under Maslow's "Hierarchy of Needs," as parallel spiritual and psychological ladders, is really a fair interpretation? In that regard, it is worth reading firsthand what Maslow himself said in his (1969) article, "Theory Z" (reprinted in Maslow's basic text on Transpersonal Psychology, The Farther Reaches of Human Nature, NY: Viking, [1972]).

Maslow describes in detail in that text those rare people who do in fact climb to the top of his psychological pyramid, those who give unconditionally of themselves to better the world, under a thesis that he referred to as "Theory Z," or again as "transcenders." He then describes such true "transcenders" as follows:

...They speak more easily, normally, naturally, and unconsciously the language of Being (B-language), the language of poets, of mystics, of seers, of profoundly religious men...

...They perceive intuitively or sacrally (i.e., the sacred within the secular), or they see the sacredness in all things at the same time that they also see them at the practical, everyday D-level....

---

* * * *

...Not only are such people lovable as are all of the most self-actualizing people, but they are also more

awe-inspiring, more "unearthly," more godlike, more "saintly"..., more easily revered...

---

*   *   *   *

...I have a vague impression that the transcenders are less "happy" than the healthy ones. They can be more ecstatic, more rapturous, and experience greater heights of "happiness" (a too weak word) than the happy and healthy ones. But I sometimes get the impression that they are as prone and maybe more prone to a kind of cosmic sadness or B-sadness over the stupidity of people, their self-defeat, their blindness, their cruelty to each other, their shortsightedness... Perhaps this is a price these people have to pay for their direct seeing of the beauty of the world, of the saintly possibilities in human nature, of the non-necessity of so much of human evil, of the seemingly obvious necessities for a good world.... Any transcender could sit down and in five minutes write a recipe for peace...

---

*   *   *   *

...Transcenders are in principle (I have no data) more apt to be profoundly "religious" or "spiritual" in either the theistic or nontheistic sense. Peak experiences and other transcendent experiences are in effect also to be seen as "religious or spiritual" experiences...

"Then said Jesus, Father, forgive them; for they know not what they do."
(Luke 23:34) © Carl Bloch

Thus, before he died, this ardent atheist, Abraham Maslow, in promulgating the highest level of his "Hierarchy of Needs," had inadvertently become, in practice, a proponent of the best principles of Christianity.

⬥

One final life practice that we must discuss, a concept that truly fulfills the Beatitudes – perhaps it should be considered a ninth Beatitude in practice – and which is also tied directly into the psychological health of living a truly Christian life, is the Faith's stirring and revolutionary concept of forgiveness:

Then Peter came to Jesus and asked "Lord, how many times shall I forgive my brothers and sisters who rise against me? Up to seven times?

Jesus answered, "I tell you, not seven times, but seventy-seven times."

- MATTHEW 18:21-22

Studies show that when people consider forgiveness

of others, circuits in the human limbic system (the brain areas near the cortex, which controls basic emotions including pleasure) light up on brain scans.

In a landmark study, in 2003, the University of Michigan published the results of a study of 1,500 Americans concerning their practices of forgiveness (of others, of self, and even if they thought they had experienced forgiveness by God). The physical and mental health of those people were then measured. Middle-aged and senior people were found to have forgiven others more often, and also felt more forgiven by God. Positive health was found to have a strong correlation with the forgiveness of others. Those middle-aged and older persons who practice forgiveness reported greater life satisfaction and fewer symptoms of psychological distress. The study further found that interpersonal forgiveness often has its roots in the unique Christian doctrine of unconditional forgiveness by God:

Based on findings from our qualitative studies, we hypothesized that people are more likely to forgive others unconditionally if they believe God has forgiven them for their own transgressions...The data... reveal that older people who feel they are forgiven by God are approximately two and a half times more likely to feel that transgressors should be forgiven unconditionally than older people who do not feel they are forgiven by God.

- NEAL KRAUSE AND CHRISTOPHER G. ELLISON. "FOR-GIVENESS BY GOD, FORGIVENESS OF OTHERS, AND PSY-CHOLOGICAL WELL-BEING IN LATE LIFE." J SCI STUDY RELIG. 42.1 (2003).

In short, the study concluded that it is the adoption of a religion (such as Christianity) that emphasizes God's forgiveness, that is the critical factor leading us to forgive our fellow beings. It also found that the ability to forgive may in fact be the most important asset to be cultivated to enjoy a joyous long life. For example, it has rightly been said that, "A happy marriage is a union of two good forgivers."

TODAY: "IN STUDY AFTER STUDY, RESULTS INDICATE THAT PEOPLE WHO ARE FORGIVING TEND TO NOT ONLY HAVE LESS STRESS BUT BETTER RELATIONSHIPS [AND] FEWER GENERAL HEALTH PROBLEMS..."

-FRED LARKIN, PH.D., DIRECTOR OF STANFORD UNIVERSITY FORGIVENESS PROJECT

The bottom line then is this: contrary to Hitchens' view that "religion poisons everything," both psychological studies and one of history's greatest psychologists, Maslow himself, concluded that independent of whether or not God exists, "the highest levels of development of humanness is ... a sense of obligation [to the Divine]," particularly a belief in divine forgiveness.

Ultimately, after reviewing the historical evidence, the ultimate conundrum that both believers and non-believers are left to ponder is this: did Christians bring the remarkable changes we have described in this book to the world through the intersection of human creativity and Divine Providence? Or does devout Christianity, by inspiring sacrificial conduct, generate outcomes that mimic the divine through a type of "placebo" effect, as a form of ratification of Alexander Pope's, "To err is human; to forgive, divine." After all, as Thomas Merton put it, truly knowing God is like realizing that "one holds the winning ticket in a cosmic sweepstakes."

Put another way, each reader must decide for him or herself whether or not Christianity is divinely inspired, as Christians like myself believe, or merely in certain instances so psychologically transcendent as to be divinely inspirational, as in the Maslow sense. One can be persuaded by William Hutchison Murray's "providential theory" of progress which follows, as I am, or not, as you please:

Until one is committed, there is hesitancy, the chance to draw back, always ineffectiveness. Concerning all acts of initiative (and creation), there is one elementary truth that ignorance of which kills countless ideas and splendid plans: that the moment one definitely commits oneself, then Providence moves too. All sorts of things occur to help one that would never otherwise have occurred. A whole stream of events issues from the decision, raising in one's favor all manner of unforeseen incidents and meetings and material assistance, which no man could have dreamed would have come his way. Whatever you can do, or dream you can do, begin it. Boldness has genius, power, and magic in it. Begin it now.

- WILLIAM HUTCHISON MURRAY, THE SCOTTISH HIMA-
LAYAN EXPEDITION (1951).

But, either way, what no one can say truthfully, factually, is that Christianity has not (and does not) matter. Rather, now, for the contributions to world civilization that you have seen documented in this book, I hope you, Christians and non-Christians alike, will join me in saying to Christianity, especially Beatitudinal Christianity, "Thank you."

—— CONCLUSION ——

CHRISTIANITY MATTERS.

CHRISTIANITY MATTERS.

THE BEATITUDES MATTER.

A as you have seen, what we can refer to as 'Beatitudinal Christianity,' or similarly as 'New Testament Christianity,' has played a powerful historical role in civilizing our world.

Today, Christianity itself is at a distinct crossroads. Politically powerful conservative evangelical forces, particularly in certain regions of the United States, have lifted into ascendancy a distinct form of Christianity that Christ would not even recognize, centered upon the rigid rules of the Ten Commandments, not the inner grace and forgiveness of the Beatitudes, and thinly veiled nativism and racism. These 'Christians' promote widespread access to automatic weapons, glorified violence and militarism, and the primacy of money-dominated sports leagues and material gain. In the marketplace of ideas, these 'Old Testament Christians' are thus now, as a group, clashing with 'Beatitudinal Christians,' damaging Christianity's reputation, and holding back, not promoting, true spiritual progress.

Indeed, the symbolic juxtaposition of Abraham Lincoln quoting the Sermon on the Mount just before his death, on the one hand, and John Wilkes Booth engaging in gun violence while wearing a Christian medal, on the other, personifies the ideological confusion in the American Christian community that still exists today.

At the same time, the Catholic Church (especially in America), despite being engaged in admirable acts of charity, is to a significant extent bleeding off and failing to retain its female and younger membership – particularly among millennials – by continuing to fill its leadership roles solely based upon gender.

As the true Christian message becomes muted by these clashing trends, David Bentley Hart predicts the future of modernity to be not only post-Christian, but irreversibly so:

For centuries the Christian story shaped and suffused our civilization; now, however, slowly but relentlessly, another story is replacing it, and any attempt to reverse that process is probably futile. We are not pagans; we are not moved by their desires or disquieted by their uncertainties. We live after the age of Christendom, and cultures do not easily turn back to beliefs of which they have tired or with which they have become disenchanted.

- HART, ATHEIST DELUSIONS, SUPRA.

There are statistics to support his case. Christian church attendance in Europe is abysmally low, church attendance in most developed countries is declining, and around the world Christians too often live under duress politically and, at times, physically. Since 1955, church attendance among American Catholics has dropped from 75% to about 45%, and the number of former Catholics is close to ten percent of the U.S. population – a number so large, it would qualify as the second largest religion.

Meanwhile, as Professor Hart has observed, there would appear to be no let-up from those whose dogma insists upon ending the experience of Faith, though they provide no convincing empirical proof whatsoever that what they would replace it with would serve as an effective source of moral imperatives:

Western atheism is something quite novel in human history: not mere personal unbelief, and not merely the eccentric doctrine of one or another small philosophical sect, but a conscious ideological, social, and philosophical project, with a broad popular constituency—a cause, a dogma, a metaphysics, a system of values.

- DAVID BENTLEY HART, THE EXPERIENCE OF GOD: BEING, CONSCIOUSNESS, BLISS (2013).

So what comes next? Are we to let this powerful Christian revolution stagnate, or even die?

Are we to let the motivation for the work of Fabiola in creating hospitals be forgotten and in vain? Are we to let the theology behind the reforms of William Wilberforce in ending slavery be forgotten and in vain? Are we to let the human rights reforms in the form of the Geneva Convention of Henry Dunant be in vain as new forms of torture proliferate (and are even used against Christians) in the Middle East? Did Sister Marianne Cope dedicate her life to the care of lepers only to now see her own religion itself become critically ill? Did Sister Dorothy Stang recite out loud the Beatitudes over ringing gun shots in vain – because in the future, fewer and fewer people will be listening to those words, as they are drowned out by gun shots around the world?

The answer has to be no.

For Christianity to thrive today in America, especially in the wake of the Church sex abuse scandal, it must re-establish its reputation not only for its spiritual purity, but also for its practical value.

This is where you come in.

If Christianity is to retain its religious leadership role, not to mention its civilizing role, then surely you (and I) must insist that the Church do some things differently. I would suggest that we must mark the words of Tyler Wigg-Stevenson in <u>The World is Not Ours to Save: Finding the Freedom to Do Good</u> (2013):

*The current context of cultural and religious pluralism magnifies this development. After the disintegration of Christendom – a historical apparatus that gave cultural pride of place to Christianity – Christian truth claims cannot be taken for granted or simply asserted using logical apologetics. **Rather, the truth of the faith appears to stand or fall based on its goodness, as shown in the lives of those who claim it.** This means that Christianity has something to prove, and this in turn has generated a faith that is focused outward, engaged with culture, concerned with authenticity and activist in its orientation. [Emphasis added].*

As for a specific agenda, based upon Beatitudinal values, Philip Gulley suggests one for American Christianity to adopt in his excellent book *If the Church Were Christian: Rediscovering the Values of Jesus* (2011):

If the church were Christian, Jesus would be a model for living, not an object of worship.

If the church were Christian, affirming our potential would be more important than condemning our brokenness.

If the church were Christian, reconciliation would be valued over judgment.

If the church were Christian, gracious behavior would be more important than right belief.

If the church were Christian, inviting questions would be more important than supplying answers.

If the church were Christian, encouraging exploration would be more important than communal uniformity.

If the church were Christian, meeting needs would be more important than maintaining institutions.

If the church were Christian, peace would be more important than power.

If the church were Christian, it would care more about love and less about sex.

If the church were Christian, this life would be more important than the afterlife.

The answer is therefore simply that the Church, including the laity, must return wholeheartedly, as in the early centuries, to Beatitudinal Christianity – not only in tone, but also in actions, and not only through its leadership and administrative structures, but through gender-neutral, direct, lay, servant-focused volunteerism:

- **Thus, every Christian church in the world should set up, over the next five years, youth or adult volunteer 'Beatitudes in Action' Committees related to care for the lonely or sick, support for the poor, or promoting dignity, equality and justice.**

- **Also, these groups must include in their primary leadership, dynamic spiritual women – a group that, as you now know from this book, has always been at the forefront of the deepest sacrifices, the most dynamic growth in and the greatest accomplishments of the Faith.**

- **Christians at all levels must speak out boldly and act to protect the environment, to end resource and health care deprivation, to limit gun violence, to oppose discrimination and to close the wealth gap. These are not just political issues; these are Christian imperatives.**

In the Catholic Church, Pope Francis has recently appointed a Catholic Church committee to consider whether women can be made deacons. They should be allowed to so serve (hopefully as a step toward their full acceptance in the Church leadership), and sisters already living a consecrated life should be among those allowed to so serve. Other Church reforms must ensure that women of faith are treated with full equality and dignity.

Only then will the purity and sincerity of Christian love give it the strength to withstand the current torrent of criticism, and to be reborn. As Winston Churchill once explained, when under attack:

The only guide to a man is his conscience; the only shield to his memory is the rectitude and sincerity of his actions. It is very imprudent to walk through life without this shield, because we are so often mocked by the failure of our hopes and the upsetting of our calculations; but with this shield, however the fates may play, we march always in the ranks of honor.

In short, to build our shield, during an era of often excessive attacks, we need to flood the planet with loving service. We must give love as the fir tree gives its scent –fully, sweetly, constantly and unconditionally. We must, as Orpheus did, drown out the destructive siren song which is the ugliness and violence that too often envelops much of contemporary life, with the far more beautiful poetry of peace shown in the Beatitudes.

And yes, even in 2016, others will still follow. In droves – just as they did two thousand years ago, when Christians, especially Christian women, for the first time, cared for the contagious sick without consideration of status, gender, ethnicity, nationality, or tribe, in the first hospitals.

Because sickness may sometimes be contagious, but nothing is more contagious than courage.

Yes, Christianity still matters. C.S. Lewis once said:

Christianity, if false, is of no importance, and if true, of infinite importance. The only thing it cannot be is moderately important.

- C.S. LEWIS, GOD IN THE DOCK: ESSAYS ON THEOLOGY AND ETHICS, 2014.

Yes, the Beatitudes always have been, and always will be, the answer.

—————— SOURCES ——————

BOOKS

Armstrong, Karen. *Fields of Blood: Religion and the History of Violence*. London: Vintage, 2015. Print.

Armstrong, Karen. *Islam: A Short History*. Modern Library Paperback ed. New York: Modern Library, 2002. Print.

Bass, Diana Butler. *A People's History of Christianity: The Other Side of the Story*. 1st HarperCollins Paperback ed. New York: HarperOne, 2010. Print.

Bays, Daniel H. *A New History of Christianity in China*. Chichester, West Sussex: Wiley-Blackwell, 2012. Print.

Benthall, Jonathan. *Returning to Religion: Why a Secular Age is Haunted by Faith*. London: I.B. Tauris, 2008. Print.

Biggs, Brooke S. *Brave Hearts, Rebel Spirits: The Spiritual Activists Handbook*. Chichester: Anita Roddick, 2003. Print.

Bonhoeffer, Dietrich. *Life Together*. New York: Harper & Row, 1954. Print.

Bonhoeffer, Dietrich. *The Cost of Discipleship*. New York: Macmillan, 1959. Print.

Broocks, Rice. *God's Not Dead: Evidence for God in an Age of Uncertainty*. Nashville: W. Publishing Group, 2013. Print.

Burleigh, Michael. *Sacred Causes: Religion and Politics from the European Dictators to Al Qaeda*. London: Harper Perennial, 2007. Print.

Burnett, Deena and Anthony Giombetti. *Fighting Back: Living Life Beyond Ourselves: Fighting Back: Defining Moments in the Life of an American Hero*. Longwood, Fla.: Advantage Books, 2006. Print.

Butler, Alban, and Michael J. Walsh. *Butler's Lives of the Saints:*

Concise Edition. 1st HarperCollins Paperback ed. San Francisco: HarperSanFrancisco, 1991. Print.

Cahill, Thomas. *How the Irish Saved Civilization: The Untold Story of Ireland's Heroic Role from the Fall of Rome to the Rise of Medieval Europe*. New York: Anchor Books, Doubleday, 1996. Print.

Callahan, David. *The Cheating Culture: Why More Americans Are Doing Wrong to Get Ahead*. 1st Harvest ed. Orlando, Fla.: Harcourt, 2004. Print.

Campbell, Joseph and Safron Rossi. *Goddesses: Mysteries of the Feminine Divine*. Novato, Cal.: Joseph Campbell Foundation: New World Library, 2013. Print.

Carmichael, Amy. *Things As They Are: Mission Work in Southern India*. London: Morgan and Scott, 1905. Print.

Carroll, James. *Constantine's Sword: The Church and the Jews: A History*. 1st Mariner Books ed. Boston: Houghton Mifflin, 2002. Print.

Carter, Jimmy. *A Call to Action: Women, Religion, Violence, and Power*. New York: Simon & Schuster, 2014. Print.

Carter, Jimmy. *A Full Life: Reflections at Ninety*. 1st Simon & Schuster hardcover ed. New York: Simon & Schuster, 2015. Print.

Cavanaugh, William T. *The Myth of Religious Violence: Secular Ideology and the Roots of Modern Conflict*. Oxford: Oxford University Press, 2009. Print.

Chatterjee, Aroup. *Mother Teresa: The Untold Story*. New Delhi: Fingerprint!, 2016. Print.

Cochrane, Arthur C. *The Church's Confession Under Hitler*. 2nd ed. Eugene, OR: Pickwick Publications/Wipf and Stock, 2009. Print.

Collins, Paul. *The Modern Inquisition: Seven Prominent Catholics and Their Struggles with the Vatican*. Woodstock, NY:

Overlook Press, 2002. Print.

Connor, Charles P. *Classic Catholic Converts*. San Francisco: Ignatius Press, 2001. Print.

Crocker, H.W. *Triumph: The Power and the Glory of the Catholic Church: A 2,000-Year History*. 1st ed. Roseville, Cal.: Forum, 2001. Print.

Daniel-Rops, Henri. *The Church in the Seventeenth Century, Vol. 1*. Garden City, NY: Doubleday, 1965.

D'Arcy, Mary R. *The Saints of Ireland: A Chronological Account of the Lives and Works of Ireland's Saints and Missionaries at Home and Abroad*. St. Paul: Irish American Cultural Institute, 1974. Print.

Dawkins, Richard. *The God Delusion*. 1st Mariner Books ed. Boston: Houghton Mifflin, 2008. Print.

Dawson, Christopher. *Religion and the Rise of Western Culture*. New York: Doubleday, 1991. Print.

Donohue, William A. *Why Catholicism Matters: How Catholic Virtues Can Reshape Society in the 21st Century*. 1st ed. New York: Image, 2012. Print.

Douglas-Klotz, Neil. *Prayers of the Cosmos: Reflections on the Original Meaning of Jesus's Words*. 1st HarperCollins Paperback ed. New York: HarperOne, 1994. Print.

Douthat, Ross. *Bad Religion: How We Became a Nation of Heretics*. 1st Free Press hardcover ed. New York: Free Press, 2012. Print.

D'Souza, Dinesh. *What's so Great About Christianity*. Carol Stream, Ill.: Tyndale House Publishers, 2008. Print.

Dunant, Henry. *A Memory of Solferino*. Washington, D.C: American National Red Cross, 1959. Print.

Eliot, T S. *Christianity and Culture: The Idea of a Christian Society and Notes Towards the Definition of Culture*. New York: Harcourt, Brace, 1949. Print.

Eusebius. *Ecclesiastical History*. Cambridge, Mass.: Harvard University Press, 1965. Print.

Ferguson, Niall. *Civilization: The West and the Rest*. New York: Penguin Press, 2011. Print.

Ferry, Luc. *A Brief History of Thought: A Philosophical Guide to Living*. New York: Harper Perennial, 2011. Print.

Fialka, John J. *Sisters: Catholic Nuns and the Making of America*. New York: St. Martin's Press, 2003. Print.

Fox, Emmett. *The Sermon on the Mount: The Key to Success in Life; And, The Lord's Prayer, An Interpretation*. 1st Harper-Collins Paperback ed. New York: HarperOne, 1989. Print.

Francis, Pope. *Amoris Laetitia: The Joy of Love*. Frederick, Maryland: Word Among Us, 2016. 46-47. Print.

Fredriksen, Paula. *From Jesus to Christ: The Origins of the New Testament Images of Jesus*. 2nd ed. New Haven, Conn.: Yale University Press, 2000. Print.

Furlong, Paul and David Curtis. *The Church Faces the Modern World: Rerum Novarum and its Impact*. Winteringham: Earlsgate Press, 1994. Print.

Garlow, James L. *A Christian's Response to Islam*. 2nd ed. Colorado Springs, Colo.: Victor, 2005.

Garratt, Alfred C. *Myths in Medicine and Old-Time Doctors*. New York and London: G.P. Putnam's Sons, 1884. Print.

Gbowee, Leymah and Carol Mithers. *Mighty Be Our Powers: How Sisterhood, Prayer, and Sex Changed a Nation at War: A Memoir*. New York: Beast Books, 2011. Print.

Gibbon, Edward, and Hans-Friedrich Mueller. *The Decline and Fall of the Roman Empire*. Modern Library Paperback ed. New York: Modern Library, 2003. Print.

Gladwell, Malcolm. *David and Goliath: Underdogs, Misfits, and the Art of Battling Giants*. 1st ed. New York: Little, Brown and Company, 2013. Print.

Goettner-Abendroth, Heide. *Societies of Peace: Matriarchies Past, Present and Future: Selected Papers, First World Congress on Matriarchal Studies, 2003, Second World Congress on Matriarchal Studies, 2005*. Toronto: Inanna Publications, 2009. Print.

Goldhagen, Daniel J. *Hitler's Willing Executioners: Ordinary Germans and the Holocaust*. New York: Knopf, 1996. Print.

Groome, Thomas H. *What Makes Us Catholic: Eight Gifts for Life*. San Francisco: HarperSanFrancisco, 2002. Print.

Guelich, Robert A. *The Sermon on the Mount: A Foundation for Understanding*. Waco, Tex.: Word Books, 1982. Print.

Gulley, Philip. *If the Church Were Christian: Rediscovering the Values of Jesus*. New York: HarperOne, 2010. Print.

Haidt, Jonathan. *The Righteous Mind: Why Good People Are Divided by Politics and Religion*. 1st Vintage Books ed. New York: Vintage Books, 2013. Print.

Halberstam, David. *Firehouse*. 1st ed. New York: Hyperion, 2002. Print.

Harris, Sam. *The End of Faith: Religion, Terror, and the Future of Reason*. New York: W.W. Norton & Co, 2004. Print.

Hart, David B. *Atheist Delusions: The Christian Revolution and Its Fashionable Enemies*. New Haven, Conn.: Yale University Press, 2009. Print.

Hart, David B. *The Experience of God: Being, Consciousness, Bliss*. New Haven, Conn.: Yale University Press, 2013. Print.

Hart, Michael H. *The 100: A Ranking of the Most Influential Persons in History*. Rev. ed. Secaucus, N.J.: Carol Publishing Group, 1998. Print.

Hayward, Susan and Katherine Marshall. *Women, Religion, and Peacebuilding: Illuminating the Unseen*. Washington, D.C.: United States Institute of Peace Press, 2015. Print.

Hitchens, Christopher. *God is Not Great: How Religion Poisons*

Everything. 1st ed. New York: Twelve, 2007. Print.

Ivereigh, Austen. *The Great Reformer: Francis and the Making of a Radical Pope*. 1st ed. New York: Henry Holt and Company, 2014. Print.

Jefferson, Thomas. *The Jefferson Bible: The Life and Morals of Jesus of Nazareth*. Boston: Beacon Press, 1989. Print.

Jenkins, Philip. *Pedophiles and Priests: Anatomy of a Contemporary Crisis*. New York: Oxford University Press, 1996. Print.

Jenkins, Philip. *The Lost History of Christianity: The Thousand-Year Golden Age of the Church in the Middle East, Africa, and Asia—and How it Died*. 1st ed. New York: HarperOne, 2008. Print.

Jenkins, Philip. *The New Anti-Catholicism: The Last Acceptable Prejudice*. New York: Oxford University Press, 2003. Print.

Johnson, Paul. *A History of Christianity*. 1st Touchstone ed. New York: Simon & Schuster, 1995. Print.

Johnson, Paul. *Heroes: From Alexander the Great and Julius Caesar to Churchill and De Gaulle*. New York: HarperCollins, 2007. Print.

Jones, E. Stanley. *The Christ of The Mount: A Working Philosophy of Life*. New York: Abingdon Press, 1931. Print.

Keller, Timothy J. *The Reason for God: Belief in an Age of Skepticism*. 1st Riverhead trade paperback ed. New York: Riverhead Books, 2009. Print.

Kwitny, Jonathan. *Man of the Century: The Life and Times of Pope John Paul II*. New York: Henry Holt and Co., 1997. Print.

Lewis, C.S. *The Screwtape Letters: With, Screwtape Proposes a Toast*. San Francisco: HarperSanFrancisco, 2001. Print.

Lewis, C.S., and Walter Hooper. *God in the Dock: Essays on Theology and Ethics*. Grand Rapids, Mich.: Wm. B. Eerdmans

Publsihing Co., 2014. Print.

Locke, John. *Two Treatises on Government*. London: Awnsham Churchill, 1690. Print.

Longman, Jere. *Among the Heroes: The Story of Flight 93 and the Passengers and Crew Who Fought Back*. London: Simon & Schuster, 2002. Print.

Lutzer, Erwin W. *Hitler's Cross*. Chicago: Moody, 1995. Print.

Mandela, Nelson. *Long Walk to Freedom: The Autobiography of Nelson Mandela*. Boston: Little, Brown, 1994. Print.

Mansfield, Stephen. *Lincoln's Battle with God: A President's Struggle with Faith and What It Meant for America*. Nashville: Thomas Nelson, 2012. Print.

Mariani, Paul P. *Church Militant: Bishop Kung and Catholic Resistance in Communist Shanghai*. Cambridge, Mass.: Harvard University Press, 2011. Print.

Maslow, Abraham H. *The Farther Reaches of Human Nature*. New York: Viking Press, 1972. Print.

McLaren, Brian D. *A New Kind of Christianity: Ten Questions That Are Transforming the Faith*. 1st ed. New York: HarperOne., 2010. Print.

Merton, Thomas. *The Seven Storey Mountain: An Autobiography of Faith*. 50th Anniversary ed., 1st Harvest ed. San Diego: Harcourt Brace, 1999. Print.

Merton, Thomas. *Zen and the Birds of Appetite*. New York: New Directions, 1968. Print.

Merton, Thomas, and Kathleen Deignan. *A Book of Hours*. Notre Dame, Ind: Sorin Books, 2007. Print.

Metaxas, Eric. *Seven Men: And the Secret of Their Greatness*. Nashville: Thomas Nelson, 2013. Print.

Metaxas, Eric. *Miracles: What They Are, Why They Happen, and How They Can Change Your Life*. New York: Dutton/Penguin Group USA, 2014. Print.

Micklethwait, John, and Adrian Wooldridge. *God Is Back: How the Global Revival of Faith Is Changing the World*. Paperback ed. New York: Penguin Books, 2010. Print.

Moses, Paul. *The Saint and the Sultan: The Crusades, Islam, and Francis of Assisi's Mission of Peace*. New York: Doubleday Religion, 2009. Print.

Moynahan, Brian. *The Faith: A History of Christianity*. 1st ed. New York: Doubleday, 2002. Print.

Murray, William H. *The Scottish Himalayan Expedition*. London: Dent, 1951. Print.

Nietzsche, Friedrich, and Walter Kaufmann. *The Will to Power*. New York: Random House, 1968. Print.

Pinker, Steven. *The Better Angels of Our Nature: Why Violence Has Declined*. New York: Penguin Books, 2012. Print.

Pramuk, Christopher. *Sophia: The Hidden Christ of Thomas Merton*. Collegeville, Minn.: Liturgical Press, 2009. Print.

Putnam, Robert D. and David E. Campbell. *American Grace: How Religion Divides and Unifies Us*. 1st Simon & Schuster Paperback ed. New York: Simon & Schuster, 2012. Print.

Risse, Guenter B. *Mending Bodies, Saving Souls: A History of Hospitals*. New York: Oxford University Press, 1999. Print.

Robinson, Daniel N. *The Great Ideas of Philosophy: [course Guidebook]*. 2nd ed. Chantilly, VA: The Teaching Company, 2004. Print.

Shuster, Eric. *Where Are the Christians?: The Unrealized Potential of a Divided Religion*. Springville, UT: Plain Sight Publishing, 2013. Print.

Stark, Rodney. *America's Blessings: How Religion Benefits Everyone, Including Atheists*. West Conshohocken, PA: Templeton Press, 2012. Print.

Stark, Rodney. *Discovering God: The Origins of the Great Religions and the Evolution of Belief*. New York: HarperOne,

2007. Print.

Stark, Rodney. *God's Battalions: The Case for the Crusades.* 1st HarperCollins Paperback ed. New York: HarperOne, 2010. Print.

Stark, Rodney. *How the West Won: The Neglected Story of the Triumph of Modernity.* Wilmington, Delaware: ISI Books, 2014. Print.

Stark, Rodney. *The Rise of Christianity: How the Obscure, Marginal Jesus Movement Became the Dominant Religious Force in the Western World in a Few Centuries.* 1st HarperCollins Paperback ed. New York: HarperOne, 1997. Print.

Stark, Rodney. *The Triumph of Christianity: How the Jesus Movement Became the World's Largest Religion.* New York: HarperOne, 2011. Print.

Stark, Rodney, and Katie E. Corcoran. *Religious Hostility: A Global Assessment of Hatred and Terror.* Waco, Tex.: ISR Books, 2014. Print.

Stark, Rodney, and Xiuhua Wang. *A Star in the East: The Rise of Christianity in China.* West Conshohocken, PA: Templeton Press, 2015. Print.

Stearns, Richard. *The Hole in Our Gospel.* Nashville, TN: Thomas Nelson, 2009. Print.

Taunton, Larry A. *The Grace Effect: How the Power of One Life can Reverse the Corruption of Unbelief.* Nashville, TN: Thomas Nelson, 2011. Print.

Thurman, Howard. *The Mood of Christmas and Other Celebrations.* Richmond, Ind: Friends United Press, 1985. Print.

Watson, Peter. *The Age of Atheists: How We Have Sought to Live Since the Death of God.* 1st Simon & Schuster Trade Paperback ed. New York: Simon & Schuster, 2014. Print.

Van Biema, David. *Mother Teresa: The Life and Works of a Modern Saint.* New York: Time Books, 2016. Print.

Wigg-Stevenson, Tyler. *The World is Not Ours to Save: Finding the Freedom to Do Good*. Downers Grove, Ill.: InterVarsity Press, 2013. Print.

Wilberforce, William and Bob Beltz. *Real Christianity*. Bethany House ed. Bloomington, Minn.: Bethany House, 2014. Print.

Wills, Garry. *Why I Am A Catholic*. Boston: Houghton Mifflin, 2002. Print.

Wilson, A. N. *Jesus: A Life*. 1st American ed. New York: W.W. Norton & Company, 1992. Print.

Wilson, Bill. *Alcoholics Anonymous: The Story of How Many More Than One Hundred Men Have Recovered from Alcoholism*. New York: Works Pub. Co, 1939. Print.

Wright, Bradley R. E. *Christians Are Hate-Filled Hypocrites and Other Lies You've Been Told: A Sociologist Shatters Myths from the Secular and Christian Media*. Minneapolis, Minn: Bethany House, 2010. Print.

Zagano, Phyllis. *Twentieth-Century Apostles: Contemporary Spirituality in Action*. Collegeville, Minn.: Liturgical Press, 1999. Print.

SELECTED PERIODICALS, STUDIES, LECTURES AND WEBSITES

Ash, Timothy G. "The Greatest Political Actor of Our Time Leaves Us the Challenge of Moral Globalization." *The Guardian*. 4 April 2005. Web. 11 May 2016.

Arnstein, Margaret G. "Florence Nightingale's Influence on Nursing." Bull. N.Y. Acad. Med. 32.7 (July 1956): 540. Web. 11 May 2016.

Bader, William D. "Some Thoughts on Blackstone, Precedent, and Originalism." *Vermont Law Review* 19.5 (1994-1995).

Web. 11 May 2016.

Bays, Daniel H. "Chinese Protestant Christianity Today." *China Quarterly*. (2003): 488-504. Print.

Beal-Preston, Rosie. "The Christian Contribution to Medicine." *Triple Helix*. (Spring 2000): 9-14. Web. 11 May 2016.

Brock, Sebastian. "The Holy Spirit as Feminine in Early Syriac Literature." In *After Eve*, ed. Janice Martin Soskice. London: Collins Marshall Pickering, 1990. Web. 18 August 2016. <http://www.womenpriests.org/theology/brock.asp>.

Brown, Andrew. "China doesn't want to suppress Christianity – just control it." *The Guardian*. 30 July 2015. Web. 6 September 2016.

Brown, Philip H. and Tierney, Brian. "Religion and Subjective Well-Being among the Elderly in China." *Journal of Socio-Economics* 38.2 (2009): 310-319. Web. 6 September 2016.

Cook, Douglas. "Sir William Blackstone: A Life and Legacy Set Apart for God's Work." *Regent University Law Review* 13 (2000-2001): 169. Web. 18 August 2016.

Darton, Eric. "The Evolution of the Mission and Design of the Hospital." *EricDarton.net: Essays, Tales & Sounds*. Originally commissioned by *Metropolis* magazine. (October 1996). Web. 11 May 2016.

Day, Dorothy. "Letter on Hospices." *The Catholic Worker*, Jan. 1948: 2, 8. Web. 18 August 2016. < http://www.catholicworker.org/dorothyday/articles/183.pdf>.

Duncan, Bruce. "The Struggle to Develop a Just War Tradition in the West." Australian Catholic Social Justice Council, 8 April 2003. Web. 29 September 2016. <www.socialjustice.catholic.org.au/files/Discussion-guides/2003-the-struggle-to-develop-a-just-war-tradition-in-the-west.pdf>.

Eisner, Manuel. "Long-Term Historical Trends in Violent

Crime." *Crime and Justice* 30 (2003): 83-142. Web.

Francis. *"Laudato Si"* [Encyclical Letter on Care for Our Common Home]. http://w2.vatican.va/content/francesco/en/encyclicals/documents/papa-francesco_20150524_enciclica-laudato-si.html

Gandhi, M. K. "Ceylon Memories: Things of the Spirit." *Young India* 9.50 (December 22, 1927): 426. Web. 10 May 2016.

Gandhi, M. K and Ramananda Chatterjee, ed. "What Jesus Means to Gandhiji." *The Modern Review (A Monthly Review and Miscellany)* 70 (October 1941): 408. Web. 11 May 2016.

Gerney, Arkadi, Chelsea Parsons and Charles Posner. "America Under the Gun: A 50-State Analysis of Gun Violence and Its Link to Weak State Gun Laws." *Center for American Progress* (2013). Web. 10 May 2016.

"Global Study on Homicide." *United Nations Office on Drugs and Crime* (2011): 10. Web. 10 May 2016.

Gobry, Pascal-Emmanuel. "Can Christianity save China?" *The Week*. 14 July 2016. Web. 6 September 2016.

Hernandez, Javier C. "China Sentences Hu Shigen, Democracy Advocate, to 7 Years in Prison." *The New York Times.* 3 August 2016. Web. 6 September 2016.

Huang, Jinbo. "Being Christians in Urbanizing China: The Epistemological Tensions of the Rural Churches in the City." *Current Anthropology* 55.S10 (December 2014): S238-S247. Print.

King, Martin Luther, Jr. "Letter from a Birmingham Jail." The First Version. *The Love All People Institute*. 16 April 1963. Web. 11 May 2016. <http://www.loveallpeople.org/letterfromthebirminghamcityjail.html>.

Koltko-Rivera, Mark E. "Rediscovering the Later Version of Maslow's Hierarchy of Needs: Self-Transcendence and Opportunities for Theory, Research and Unification." *Review of General Psychology* 10.4 (2006): 302-317. Web. 10 May 2016.

Krause, Neal, and Christopher G. Ellison. "Forgiveness by God, Forgiveness of Others, and Psychological Well-Being in Late Life." *Journal for the scientific study of religion* 42.1 (2003): 77–94. Web. 10 May 2016.

Jefferson, Thomas. "Thomas Jefferson to Benjamin Rush, April 21, 1803, with Syllabus of an Estimate of the Merit of the Doctrines of Jesus, with Copies; Partial Transcription Available." 21 April 1803. MS. Lib. of Cong., Washington, D.C. *Lib. of Cong.* Web. 11 May 2016.

"Jesuits and the Situation of Women in Church and Civil Society." *General Congregation 34* (1995): Decree 14. Web. 30 August 2016. <http://www.xavier.edu/jesuitresource/jesuit-a-z/Decree-14.cfm>.

Maibach, E., Leiserowitz, A., Roser-Renouf, C., Myers, T., Rosenthal, S. & Feinberg, G. "The Francis Effect: How Pope Francis Changed the Conversation about Global Warming." George Mason University and Yale University. Fairfax, VA: George Mason University Center for Climate Change Communication (2015). Web. 11 May 2016.

Maslow, Abraham H. "A Theory of Human Motivation." *Psychological Review* 50. (1943): 370-396. Web. 10 May 2016. (Internet Resource *Classics in the History of Psychology* developed by Christopher D. Green, York University, Toronto, Ontario: <http://psychclassics.yorku.ca/Maslow/motivation.htm>.

Melchior, Jillian Kay. "Charity Begins in China." *The Weekly Standard.* 3 December 2012. 6 September 2016.

Nelson, Lynn H. "The Rise of Universities." *WWW Virtual Library.* Web. 11 May 2016. <http://www.vlib.us/medieval/lectures/universities.html>.

"The Nobel Peace Prize 1984 - Presentation Speech". *Nobelprize. org.* Nobel Media AB 2014. Web. 11 May 2016. <http://www.nobelprize.org/nobel_prizes/peace/laureates/1984/presentation-speech.html>.

Paul, Gregory S. "Cross-National Correlations of Quantifiable Societal Health with Popular Religiosity and Secularism." *Journal of Religion & Society* 7 (2005). Web. 10 May 2016.

Phillips, Tom. "Anger as Christian lawyer paraded on Chinese state TV for 'confession'. *The Guardian.* 26 February 2016. Web. 6 September 2016.

Price, Cassandra. "Hospitals – A Historical Perspective." *Clearly Caring Magazine.* Christian Life Resources, 27.5 (Sept/Oct 2007): 6-7. Web. 11 May 2016.

Putnam, Robert. "American Grace." The Tanner Lectures on Human Values. Princeton University. 27-28 October 2010. Lecture.

"Religion in Everyday Life." *Pew Research Center* (April 2016). Web. 10 May 2016.

"Religious Hostilities Reach Six-Year High." *Pew Research Center* (January 2014). Web. 10 May 2016.

"Speech by M. K. Gandhi to London Missionary Society of India in 1925" recorded by Mahadev Desai in his secretary's diary *Day to Day with Gandhi*, Vol. VII, pp. 156-161. Web. 11 May 2016. <http://sfr-21.org/sources/missionary.html>.

Stark, Rodney. "Religious Effects: In Praise of "Idealistic Humbug"." *Review of Religious Research.* 41.3 (2000): 289-310. Web. 11 May 2016.

Weiss, Antonio. "China: the future of Christianity?" *The Guardian.* 28 August 2010. Web. 6 September 2016.

Wong, Alia. "When the Last Patient Dies." *The Atlantic.* 27 May 2015. Web. 18 August 2016. <http://www.theatlantic.com/health/archive/2015/05/when-the-last-patient-

dies/394163/>.

Yang, Fenggang. "When Will China Become The World's Largest Christian Country?" *Slate*. Web. 6 September 2016. < http://www.slate.com/bigideas/what-is-the-future-of-religion/essays-and-opinions/fenggang-yang-opinion>.

Zunes, Stephen. "The Role of Non-Violent Action in the Downfall of Apartheid." *The Journal of Modern African Studies*, 37.1 (1999): 137-169. Web. 30 August 2016.

PHOTO CREDITS

Anamix. *Logo AA.svg*. 2015. Own work. *Wikimedia Commons*. Wikimedia Foundation. 19 January 2015. Web. 23 May 2016. <https://commons.wikimedia.org/wiki/File:Logo_ AA.svg>, CC BY-SA 4.0.

Author Unknown. *Frances Willard.jpg*. Before 1898. The Library of Congress – American Memory. *Wikimedia Commons*. Wikimedia Foundation. Web. 3 May 2016. <https:// commons.wikimedia.org/wiki/File:Frances_Willard.jpg>, {{PD-old-70}}.

Dr. Anne Atai-Omoruto. Photo courtesy of WONCA. http://www. globalfamilydoctor.com.

Biyue. *Fr.Maximilian Kolbe 1939.jpg*. Photograph. *Wikimedia Commons*. Wikimedia Foundation. 3 December 2010. Web. 13 May 2016. <https://commons.wikimedia.org/wiki/File:- Fr.Maximilian_Kolbe_1939.jpg>, {{PD-US-not renewed and/or PD-1996}}.

Bloch, Carl Heinrich. *Christ on the Cross*. 1870. Museum of Natural History (Denmark). *Wikimedia Commons*. Wikimedia Foundation. Web. 3 May 2016. <https://commons.wikimedia.org/wiki/File:Christ_at_the_Cross_-_Cristo_en_la_

Cruz.jpg>, {{PD-old-100}}.'

Bloch, Carl Heinrich. *Jesus Christ with the Children / Let the little Children come unto Me.* 1800s. Museum of National History at Frederiksborg Castle. *Wikimedia Commons.* Wikimedia Foundation. Web. 3 May 2016. <https://commons.wikimedia.org/wiki/File:ChristwithChildren_CarlBloch.jpg>, {{PD-old-100}}.

Bloch, Carl Heinrich. *Woman at the Well.* 29 August 2009 (photographic reproduction). Chapel at Frederiksborg Palace in Copenhagen. *Wikimedia Commons.* Wikimedia Foundation. Web. 3 May 2016. <https://commons.wikimedia.org/wiki/File:Carl_Heinrich_Bloch_-_Woman_at_the_Well.jpg>, {{PD-old-70}}.

Botticelli, Sandro. *Augustine of Hippo.* Circa 1490. Church of Ognissanti, Florence, Italy. *Wikimedia Commons.* Wikimedia Foundation. Web. 3 May 2016. <https://commons.wikimedia.org/wiki/File:Augustine_of_Hippo_Sandro_Botticelli.jpg>, {{PD-old-100}}.

Bruno, Jeffrey. *Canonization 2014- The Canonization of Saint John XXIII and Saint John Paul II (14036966125).jpg.* Photograph. *Wikimedia Commons.* Wikimedia Foundation. 27 April 2014. Web. 13 May 2016. <https://commons.wikimedia.org/wiki/File:Canonization_2014_The_Canonization_of_Saint_John_XXIII_and_Saint_John_Paul_II_(14036966125).jpg>, CC BY-SA 2.0.

Cardinal Kung. Permission for use granted by the Cardinal Kung Foundation. http://www.cardinalkungfoundation.org.

Crawford, Thomas Hamilton after Joshua Reynolds. *Mezzotint portrait of English jurist William Blackstone (1723-1780).* 1930. Library of Congress Prints and Photographs Division. *Wikimedia Commons.* Wikimedia Foundation. Web. 13 May 2016. <https://commons.wikimedia.org/wiki/File:William_

Blackstone_by_Thomas_Hamilton_Crawford_after_Joshua_Reynolds.jpg>, {{PD-US}}.

Civvi-commonswiki. *Eleanor Roosevelt and Human Rights Declaration.jpg*. Photograph. *Wikimedia Commons*. Wikimedia Foundation. 23 April 2006. Web. 13 May 2016. <https://commons.wikimedia.org/wiki/File:Eleanor_Roosevelt_and_Human_Rights_Declaration.jpg>, {{PD-USGov}}.

Crivelli, Carlo. *Saint Thomas Aquinas*. 15ᵗʰ Century. National Gallery, London, United Kingdom. *Wikimedia Commons*. Wikimedia Foundation. Web. 3 May 2016. <https://commons.wikimedia.org/wiki/File:St-thomas-aquinas.jpg>, {{PD-old-100}}.

Cusifain. *0317-san-patricio.jpg*. Photograph. *Wikimedia Commons*. Wikimedia Foundation. 22 September 2010. Web. 3 May 2016. <https://commons.wikimedia.org/wiki/File:0317-san-patricio.jpg>, CC BY-SA 4.0.

DeMarsico, Dick. *Martin Luther King, Jr.* 1964. Library of Congress: New York World-Telegram & Sun Collection. *Wikimedia Commons*. Wikimedia Foundation. Web. 13 May 2016. <https://commons.wikimedia.org/wiki/File:Martin_Luther_King_Jr_NYWTS.jpg>, {{PD}}.

Dietrich Bonhoeffer. (1924). Art Resource. Staatsbibliothek zu Berlin, Stiftung Preussischer Kulturbesitz, Berlin, Germany.

Dorothy Stang. Permission for use granted by the Ohio Province of the Sisters of Notre Dame de Namur. www.sndohio.org.

Dürer, Albrecht. *Kaiser Karl der Große*. 1512. Germanisches Nationalmuseum. *Wikimedia Commons*. Wikimedia Foundation. Web. 3 May 2016. <https://commons.wikimedia.org/wiki/File:Charlemagne-by-Durer.jpg>, {{PD-old-100}}.

E. Stanley Jones. Permission for use granted by E. Stanley Jones Foundation. http://www.estanleyjonesfoundation.com.

Ejdzej. *Jerzy Popieluszko.jpg*. Photographic reproduction. *Wi-*

kimedia Commons. Wikimedia Foundation. 20 November 2006. Web. 13 May 2016. <https://commons.wikimedia.org/wiki/File:Jerzy_Popieluszko.jpg>, {{PD-US-not renewed and/or PD-1996}}.

Ferrari, Manredo. *Mutter Teresa von Kalkutta.jpg*. 1985. *Wikimedia Commons*. Wikimedia Foundation. Web. 13 May 2016. <https://commons.wikimedia.org/wiki/File:Mutter_Teresa_von_Kalkutta.jpg>, CC BY-SA 4.0.

File Upload Bot (Magnus Manske). *William-Booth-c1900.jpg*. Photograph. *Wikimedia Commons*. Wikimedia Foundation. 26 December 2011. Web. 13 May 2016. <https://commons.wikimedia.org/wiki/File:William-Booth-c1900.jpg>, {{PD-1923}}.

FireflySixtySeven. *MaslowsHierarchyofNeeds.svg*. Info Graphic. *Wikimedia Commons*. Wikimedia Foundation. 2 November 2014. Web. 3 May 2016. <https://commons.wikimedia.org/wiki/File:MaslowsHierarchyOfNeeds.svg>, CC SA-BY-4.0.

François de Tours, Simon. *Vincent de Paul*. 17th Century. *Wikimedia Commons*. Wikimedia Foundation. Web. 13 May 2016. <https://commons.wikimedia.org/wiki/File:Vincent_de_Paul.PNG>, {{PD-old-70}}.

Fred Shuttlesworth. Birmingham Library Portrait Collection, Birmingham, AL.

Gardner, Alexander. *Abraham Lincoln November 1863.jpg*. 1863. Web. 13 May 2016. <https://commons.wikimedia.org/wiki/File:Abraham_Lincoln_November_1863.jpg>, {{PD-1923}}.

Gool, Benny. *Archibishop Desmond Tutu*. Photograph. *Wikimedia Commons*. Wikimedia Foundation. Web. 13 May 2016. <https://commons.wikimedia.org/wiki/File:Archbishop-Tutu-medium.jpg>, {{PD}}.

Hawaii State Archives. *Mother Marianne in 1883, shortly before coming to Hawaii.* 1883. Mother Marianne Cope and the Sisters of St. Francis. *National Park Service – U.S. Department of the Interior.* Web. 3 May 2016. <https://www.nps.gov/kala/learn/historyculture/marianne.htm>, {{PD-1923}}.

Henner, Jean-Jacques. *Fabiola.* 1829-1905. *Wikimedia Commons.* Wikimedia Foundation. Web. 3 May 2016. <https://commons.wikimedia.org/wiki/File:Jean-Jacques_Henner_Fabiola.jpg>, {{PD-old-100}}.

Hickel, Karl Anton. *William Wilberforce.* 1794. Wilberforce House, Hull Museum, Hull City Council, Hull, United Kingdom. Web. 13 May 2016. <https://commons.wikimedia.org/wiki/File:William_wilberforce.jpg>, {{PD-1923}}.

Howell, Bertha. *Mother Jones, American labor activist.* 1902. Library of Congress Prints and Photographs Division. *Wikimedia Commons.* Wikimedia Foundation. <https://commons.wikimedia.org/wiki/File:Mother_Jones_1902-11-04.jpg>, {{PD-1923}}.

Jimmy Carter. Nov. 18, 2013. Kathmandu, Nepal. *The Carter Center.* The Carter Center. Web. 3 May 2016. <http://www.cartercenter.org/news/photos/president-jimmy-carter-nepal-election.html>

Keyes, Cornelius M. *CAESAR CHAVEZ, MIGRANT WORKERS UNION LEADER.* 1972. National Archives and Records Administration, College Park, MD. *Wikimedia Commons.* Wikimedia Foundation. Web. 13 may 2016. <https://commons.wikimedia.org/wiki/File:CAESAR_CHAVEZ,_MIGRANT_WORKERS_UNION_LEADER_-_NARA_-_544069.jpg>, {{PD-USGov}}.

Kneller, Sir Godfrey. *Portrait of John Locke.* 1779. State Hermitage Museum, St. Petersburg, Russia. *Wikimedia Commons.* Wikimedia Foundation. Web. May 3, 2016. <https://commons.wikimedia.org/wiki/File:JohnLocke.png>, {{PD-old-100}}.

1Veertje. *Florence Nightingale three quarter length.jpg.* Circa 1860. *Wikimedia Commons.* Wikimedia Foundation. Web. 13 October 2016. <https://commons.wikimedia.org/wiki/File:Florence_Nightingale_three_quarter_length.jpg>, {{PD-old-70}}.

Laurentius de Voltolina. *Liber ethicorum des Henricus de Alemannia – Henricus de Alemannia con i suoi studenti.* Second half of 14th century. Kupferstichkabinett Berlin. *Wikimedia Commons.* Wikimedia Foundation. Web. 3 May 2016. <https://commons.wikimedia.org/wiki/File:Laurentius_de_Voltolina_001.jpg>, {{PD-old-100}}.

Library of the London School of Economics and Political Science. *Nelson Mandela, 2000 (5).jpg.* 2009. *Wikimedia Commons.* Wikimedia Foundation. Web. 13 May 2016. <https://commons.wikimedia.org/wiki/File:Nelson_Mandela,_2000_(5).jpg>, {{PD}}.

Mack, Dwayne (website contributor). *Wyatt Tee Walker. BlackPast.org.* BlackPast.org. Web. 13 May 2016. <http://www.blackpast.org/aah/walker-wyatt-tee-1929>, {{PD}}.

Maire. *StBrigid.jpg.* Photograph of stained glass. St. Joseph Catholic Church in Macon, Georgia. *Wikimedia Commons.* Wikimedia Foundation. 31 January 2006. Web. 3 May 2016. <https://commons.wikimedia.org/wiki/File:Stbrigid.jpg>, {{PD-1923}}.

Materialscientist. *Cesare Beccaria 1738-1794.jpg.* Photographic reproduction. 3 July 2014. Web. 13 May 2016. <https://commons.wikimedia.org/wiki/File:Cesare_Beccaria_1738-1794.jpg>, {{PD-old-70}}.

Meister von San Vitale in Ravenna. *Empress Theodora and Her Court* (Detail from 6th-century mosaic). Basilica of San Vitale in Ravenna. *Wikimedia Commons.* Wikimedia Foundation. Web. 3 May 2016. <https://commons.wikimedia.org/wiki/File:Mosaic_of_empress_Theodora,_Ravenna,_San_Vitale,_547.jpg>, {{PD-old-100}}.

Mercury543210. *Amy Carmichael with children2.jpg*. Retouched Photograph. Heroes of Faith. *Wikimedia Commons*. Wikimedia Foundation. 18 January 2014. Web. 3 May 2016. <https://commons.wikimedia.org/wiki/File:Amy_Carmichael_with_children2.jpg>, {{PD-1923}}.

Milošević, Petar. *Mosaic of Justinianus I* – Basilica San Vitale (Ravenna).jpg. Own work. 2015. *Wikimedia Commons.* Wikimedia Foundation. Web. 13 October 2016. <https://commons.wikimedia.org/wiki/File:Mosaic_of_Justinianus_I_-_Basilica_San_Vitale_(Ravenna).jpg>, CC BY-SA 4.0.

Mladifilozof. *Basil of Caesarea.jpg*. Photographic reproduction. *Wikimedia Commons*. Wikimedia Foundation. 15 June 2008. Web. 3 May 2016. <https://commons.wikimedia.org/wiki/File:Basil_of_Caesarea.jpg>, {{PD-old-70}}.

New York World-Telegram & Sun Collection. *Dorothy Day 1934.jpg*. 1934. *Wikimedia Commons*. Wikimedia Foundation. Web. 13 May 2016. <https://commons.wikimedia.org/wiki/File:Dorothy_Day_1934.jpg>, {{PD-US-no notice}}.

Nguyen, Marie-Lan. *Children games Louvre Ma99.jpg*. Photographic reproduction of Marble, Roman artwork of 2nd century AD. Louvre Museum. *Wikimedia Commons*. Wikimedia Foundation. 4 January 2010. Web. 3 May 2016. <https://commons.wikimedia.org/wiki/File:Children_games_Louvre_Ma99.jpg>, CC BY 3.0.

Peale, Charles Willson. *Portrait of Thomas Jefferson (1743-1826)*. 1791. Independence National Historical Park, Philadelphia, Pennsylvania. *Wikimedia Commons*. Wikimedia Foundation. Web. 3 May 2016. <https://commons.wikimedia.org/wiki/File:T_Jefferson_by_Charles_Willson_Peale_1791_2.

jpg>, {{PD-old-100}}.

Portrait of Dag Hammarskjöld, Secretary-General of the United Nations. 1959. UN Photo/JO.

Randall Studio. *Sojourner Truth.* Circa 1870. National Portrait Gallery, Smithsonian Institution, London, United Kingdom. Web. 13 May 2016. <https://commons.wikimedia.org/wiki/File:Sojourner_truth_c1870.jpg>, {{PD-1923}}.

RoterRabe. *Pope Gregory VII.jpg.* Photographic reproduction. *Wikimedia Commons.* Wikimedia Foundation. 19 July 2006. Web. 3 May 2016. <https://commons.wikimedia.org/wiki/File:Pope_Gregory_VII.jpg>, {{PD-old-70}}.

Sarvodaya. *Francisco vitoria.jpg.* Photographic reproduction. *Wikimedia Commons.* Wikimedia Foundation. 1 December 2006. Web. 13 May 2016. <https://en.wikipedia.org/wiki/File:Francisco_vitoria.jpg>, {{PD-old-1923}}.

Seges. *Franciscus Suarez, S.I. (1548-1617).jpg.* Photographic reproduction. *Wikimedia Commons.* Wikimedia Foundation. 10 September 2006. Web. 13 May 2016. <https://commons.wikimedia.org/wiki/File:Franciscus_Suarez,_S.I._(1548-1617).jpg>, {{PD-old-70}}.

Soulacroix, Charles. *Image of Blessed Frédéric Ozanam in the 1800s.* Unknown date. *Wikimedia Commons.* Wikimedia Foundation. Web. 13 May 2016. <https://commons.wikimedia.org/wiki/File:Fr%C3%A9d%C3%A9ric_Ozanam.jpg >, {{PD-1923}}.

Spashett, Linda. *Stephen Langton by John Thomas.* Photographic reproduction of sculpture by John Thomas. *Wikimedia Commons.* Wikimedia Foundation. 31 July 2013. Web. 3 May 2016. <https://commons.wikimedia.org/wiki/File:John_Thomas_maquette_017.jpg>, CC BY-SA 2.5.

Stebunik. *Nicea.jpg.* 1590. Fresco in the Sistine Chapel at The Vatican. *Wikimedia Commons.* Wikimedia Foundation.

Web. 13 October 2016. <https://commons.wikimedia.org/wiki/File:Nicea.jpg>, {{PD-old-100}}.

Sweeney, Jean. "David Maloof with Leymah Gbowee." 2015. JPEG.

Tanja5. *Rosalie Rendu.jpg*. Photographic reproduction. *Wikimedia Commons*. Wikimedia Foundation. 9 April 2011. Web. 13 May 2016. <https://commons.wikimedia.org/wiki/File:Rosalie_Rendu.jpg>, {{PD-old-70}}.

Time Life Pictures. *Jean Henri Dunant.jpg*. 1901. Library of Congress Prints & Photographs Division, Washington, DC; *Wikimedia Commons*. Wikimedia Foundation. Web. 3 May 2016. <https://commons.wikimedia.org/wiki/File:Jean_Henri_Dunant.jpg>, {{PD-old-70}}.

Tissot, James. *The Sermon of the Beatitudes*. 1886-1869. From the series *The Life of Christ*, Brooklyn Museum. *Wikimedia Commons*. Web. 3 May 2016. <https://commons.wikimedia.org/wiki/File:TissotBeatitudes.JPG>, {{PD-old-100}}.

Uncredited. *Pope John Paul II on 12 August 1993 in Denver (Colorado)*. 1993. Public Papers of the Presidents of the United States – Photographic Portfolio -1993 Vol. II. *Wikimedia Commons*. Wikimedia Foundation. Web. 13 May 2016. <https://commons.wikimedia.org/wiki/File:JohannesPaul2-portrait.jpg>, {{PD-USGov}}.

van Gogh, Vincent. *The good Samaritan (after Delacroix)*. 1890. Kröller-Müller Museum. *Wikimedia Commons*. Wikimedia Foundation. Web. 3 May 2016. <https://commons.wikimedia.org/wiki/File:Vincent_Willem_van_Gogh_022.jpg>, {{PD-old-100}}.

Vatican album of the Ecumenical Council. *Pope Leo XIII*. Circa 1878. Library of Congress Prints and Photographs Division. *Wikimedia Commons*. Wikimedia Foundation. <https://commons.wikimedia.org/wiki/File:Leo_XIII.jpg>, {{PD-

1923}}.

Worthingtonlm. *Septima Clark.jpg.* 1960. Photograph. Avery Research Center Archives. *Wikimedia Commons.* Wikimedia Foundation. Web. 13 September 2016. <https://commons.wikimedia.org/wiki/File:Septima_Clark.jpg>, CC BY 4.0.

Yann. *Portrait Gandhi.jpg.* Photograph. *Wikimedia Commons.* Wikimedia Foundation. 8 July 2007. Web. 13 May 2016. <https://commons.wikimedia.org/wiki/File:Portrait_Gandhi.jpg>, {{PD-US-not renewed and/or PD-1996}}.

INDEX

A

B

C

D

E

F

G

H

I

J

K

L

M

N

R

S

T

U

V

W

Y

Z

—ACKNOWLEDGEMENTS—

During various stages of the development of this manuscript, I benefitted from the generosity of many, whether with substantive comments or with spiritual support, including my wife, Jean Sweeney, John and Sally Bassler, Warren Clark, Vito Ferrante, Nancy Geary, David Mace, Gus Nuzzolese, Dick Paterniti, the Reverend Dale Rosenberger, Professor Rodney Stark, Jay Sullivan, Rita Sweeney, Thomas Sweeney, and Brother Lawrence Syriac, S.M. of Chaminade High School.

For administrative support, great thanks are due to Christopher Cech, Brian Comberiati (for his amazing research and editing skills), Catherine O'Mara-Cherubin and Diana Russo.

—— ABOUT THE AUTHOR ——

DAVID T. MALOOF

© *Jean Sweeney*

Dave Maloof is the senior partner in Maloof Browne & Eagan LLC, an international law firm based in New York. He and his firm have handled some of the most high profile transportation casualties throughout the world and American Shipper Magazine has described Dave as "a leading attorney for shippers and cargo insurers." He has received Martindale-Hubbell's highest rating for skill and integrity, and been repeatedly named a "Super Lawyer."

Previously Dave was a highly-acclaimed investigative reporter seen on public television, uncovering government corruption, and winning major awards from the Associated Press and The Society of Professional Journalists.

He is a phi beta kappa graduate of Columbia University and a graduate of the University of Virginia Law School. Dave has taught law at St. John's University and at Roger Williams University School of Law. Dave and his family have volunteered at and sponsored athletics at a Christian refugee camp in the Middle East, and he currently holds a leadership position in a Christian international peace group, Churches for Middle East Peace. Pax Christi Metro New York annually awards the Maloof Family Young Peacebuilder Awards to the local Catholic high school students in the New York area who have done the most to promote peace. Dave and his wife Jean have two adult children and reside in Darien, Connecticut, where they attend Catholic Church, and where for a decade he organized his church's Men's Forum.

CHRISTIANITY
MATTERS.

HOW OVER TWO MILLENNIA THE MEEK AND THE MERCIFUL REVOLUTIONIZED CIVILIZATION— AND WHY IT NEEDS TO HAPPEN AGAIN

—————— By: ——————

DAVID T. MALOOF

Made in the USA
Middletown, DE
07 August 2019